DA VINCI AND THE 40 ANSWERS

A PLAYBOOK FOR CREATIVITY AND FRESH IDEAS

MARK L. FOX

PRESS

Wizard Academy Press

Austin, Texas

Copyrights Page

Printed in Canada

Wizard Academy Press
16221 Crystal Hills Drive
Austin, TX 78737
512.295.5700 voice, 512.295.5701 fax
www.WizardAcademyPress.com

Ordering Information:
To order additional copies, contact your local bookstore, visit www.WizardAcademyPress.com, or call 1.800.425.4769 Quantity discounts are available.

ISBN: 1-932226-63-X

Library of Congress Cataloging-in-Publication Data:

Fox, L. Mark.
Da vinci and the 40 answers: a playbook for creativity and fresh ideas / Mark L. Fox.
p.   cm.
ISBN 1-932226-63-X

Credits:
Cover and illustrations by Timothy McClelland

First printing: June 2008
Second printing: August 2008
Third printing: January 2009
Fourth printing: December 2009

Contents

This book as been certified by the
Rocket Science Administration for the
highest level of quality in corporate training.

www.Rocket-Science-Administration.com

Preface

This is not a "_____ for Dummies" book. This book requires you to think. Consider yourself forewarned.

When my wife decides to read, she usually picks up a Danielle Steel novel because, "it doesn't require any real thought to enjoy it." That's the same scoop I get when I ask her why she watches re-runs of "Mayberry R.F.D." and "Little House on the Prairie" before dinner every night. My wife is extremely intelligent, but after work she likes to give her mind a rest, which of course we all need to do at times.

**If you are looking for brain-dead entertainment,
then please put this book down now.**

This is a business book on creativity, innovation, marketing, and advertising. This book is intended to teach you how to run your business and life better, and the pages that follow *do* require some real thought. The ideas and concepts presented here are intended to make you think about things differently. That requires change, and for most of us, change is hard.

The Start of Something Magical

"The two of us should put a new class together." Those were Roy's first words when I answered the phone in the summer of 2006. Roy doesn't usually call me out of the blue, so I knew this was an important and serious project.

Roy H. Williams is a lifelong student of humanity, and a best-selling author many times over who spent decades asking, "What makes people do the things they do?"

Roy is also the founder of the Wizard Academy, a 21ˢᵗ Century Business School. Wizard Academy is an absolute one-of-a-kind institution. The class Roy was referring to that day, da Vinci and the 40 Answers, was developed at the academy. This course is currently taught both at the academy and at many corporations, organizations, and non-profits like yours.

My default mode is left-brain logical and Roy's is more right-brain creative. This makes for an interesting mix of personalities and perspectives in a dual-instructed course. Most people's personality and predominate mode of thinking favors one side of the brain, but both of us enjoy spending time in our other, lesser-used hemisphere. We love to spend time in both worlds, and desire for you to do the same. That is one of the aims of this book: to convince you that you need to find a better state of balance by using both sides of your brain.

The first half of the book will cover the "basics" of creativity and innovation: relearning how to play, being inspired to play, seeing the value in play, and examining the discoveries of people who were able to escape into their right brain and see beyond societal definitions of 'right' or 'wrong' thinking.

We'll examine right-brain logic through the eyes of several great thinkers: Leonardo da Vinci, Genrikh Altshuller, Buckminster Fuller, and Walt Disney. I believe these basics were the foundation for these innovators' creativity. These men may not have used my exact terms to describe the principles of creativity, or even been conscious they were using them, but I feel strongly that these basics are the common denominator of their great minds. This section should give you a solid starting point to help you understand and practice creativity and innovation.

In the second half of this book, we'll cover the "tactics": Real-life solutions to universal problems. At the end of this book, you'll understand the tactical approach to applying creativity based on the 40 Universal Answers, a series of specific techniques and perspectives. The 40 Universal Answers are founded in principles of TRIZ – the Theory of Inventive Problem Solving.

TRIZ began with Genrikh Altshuller. In his study of hundreds of thousands of patents, Altshuller determined there are only about 1,500 basic problems – and each of these problems can be solved by applying one or more of the 40 universal answers.

I have found the principles of TRIZ to be an extremely useful set of tools, but have not been totally satisfied with the way TRIZ is taught to most students and readers. TRIZ is frequently taught from a very technical point of view, which leaves most students feeling overwhelmed. The technical view is simply too complicated for most people.

One of the goals of this book is to explain the 40 Answers, or principles, as "lenses," tools you can use to view the problem or opportunity from a unique perspective. The lenses are not just beneficial for technical disciplines. The lenses translate just as well as solutions to social, economic, political, and environmental issues, as well as marketing, sales, and operations. The lenses of TRIZ can be used to solve any problem, in any part of your business and life.

My hope is to explain all these concepts with examples that are relatively easy to digest and apply. You will also see many of my own experiences described in this book as examples of times when the basics and fundamentals have worked for me.

At the end of many sections, you'll find "Words of the Wizard," insights from Wizard Academy founder and one of the top business thinkers of today, Roy H. Williams. In many cases you will realize the immediate association between Words of the Wizard and the correlating section, while in others the association is not so straightforward. This is intentional. In those cases where the connection is not transparent it will require some thought to connect the two ideas, but the connections are always there. These supplemental sections support the concept of duality. Can two different meanings of the same thing both be right? That's for you to decide.

My hope is that the information within this book inspires you to draw your own connections and conclusions, and come up with creative ideas and thoughts even beyond what I intended. I want you to learn to take your own mind to a higher level of creative thought. This book is designed to give you the ability to "think outside of the box" at the snap of the fingers. In short, you'll be handed the keys to innovation.

It is my greatest hope that *da Vinci and the 40 Answers* helps provide a foundation of both basic and tactical ways to apply creativity and innovation in your world. Onward!

Introduction

"Proverbs contradict each other.
That is the wisdom of a nation."
Stanislaw Jerzy Lec

We've all heard the expression, "think outside the box." The problem with this concept is that many people do not understand what the box is, much less how to escape this cage. When we are facing a problem, we use what we already know to determine the solution. The box is the frame of reference, the starting point for deductive reasoning.

When we deduce something, we start with a known point. Deductive reasoning applies logic that moves us from the general to the specific by using known facts, definitions, principles, and properties to reach a conclusion.

The problem with "the box" is quite simple. If you're starting with what is known and you're only willing to look at what can be extrapolated from the known, then how do you discover a thing that is not directly relative to the known? The answer to this quandary lies in duality.

Duality is the concept of equal but opposite. When we identify a thing – an idea, a concept, a principle, or a problem for example, we must be able to then step back and look at the thing we haven't been looking at. What is the opposite of this thing or this problem?

The scientific method is a problem-solving process. Scientific reasoning dictates that you begin with a hypothesis, a theory whose truth you wish to test. Experiments are designed to test the hypothesis by examining one variable at a time in order to determine whether the theory is correct or incorrect. The scientific method attempts to prove a theory by demonstrating that the theory cannot be *disproved*. Thus, if the hypothesis is correct then its opposites must be incorrect.

Niels Bohr (1885 – 1962) was a Nobel Prize-winning Danish physicist who was recognized for his contributions to our understanding of atomic structure and quantum mechanics. Bohr said that the opposite of a correct statement is an incorrect statement, which is classic duality – equal but opposite. However, Bohr seemingly contradicted this principle when he said, "But the opposite of a profound truth is often another profound truth." These are very unusual words for a scientist, but his thoughts touch on a very big idea.

Bohr was referring to the underlying principles of a truth that are mutually exclusive. Mutually exclusive principles are incompatible with one another – they cannot be reconciled. These principles are unable to both be true at the same time – if one is right, the other must be wrong. Yet Bohr says that the opposite of a profound truth is often another profound truth. Can the opposite of something that is right still be right? That depends on which side of your brain you ask.

Right Brain/Left Brain

The human brain is divided into two hemispheres: the left brain and the right brain. The hemispheres of the brain are objects of duality, equal but opposite.

Left brain logic is vertical, rational, deductive, and sequential. The left brain uses analytical thought. This hemisphere of your brain is strongly bonded to the concept of duality. To the left brain, there are only two possibilities: right and wrong.

The right brain, on the other hand, uses horizontal thought. The right brain uses pattern recognition. The right hemisphere of the brain is looking not just for the solution to the problem at hand, but for the principle that underlies the solution. It uses systemic leverage to solve not only one specific problem, but also all the other problems that are connected to the issue. The right brain allows us to pull back and understand the entire frame of reference. Our "intuition" is right-brain logic.

Your right brain has no real language functions. The languages of the right brain are not literal, legalistic, or absolute. Therefore, words that have specific definitions don't exist in the right brain.

When we go to sleep, the left brain disconnects and conscious awareness winks out; but the right brain is always awake and always churning. The right brain is looking for and trying to fit the strange pieces that it encountered during the day into a recognizable pattern. The left brain's projector, 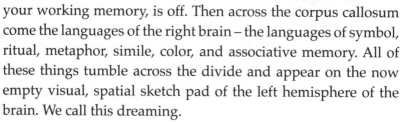 your working memory, is off. Then across the corpus callosum come the languages of the right brain – the languages of symbol, ritual, metaphor, simile, color, and associative memory. All of these things tumble across the divide and appear on the now empty visual, spatial sketch pad of the left hemisphere of the brain. We call this dreaming.

When you dream, your right brain is trying to make sense of the day. It is working to put the day's events into a recognizable pattern so that you can take the things that happened and assimilate them into your schema and outlook. Your right brain is the reason that you sometimes wake up with a new idea – something that occurred to you during the night while you were sound asleep.

The right brain has one other funny characteristic: it makes no judgment, has no morals, doesn't know fact from fiction – and the right brain doesn't care.

Think about that statement for a moment. Half of your brain, a hemisphere that is equal size in mass and complexity, doesn't know right from wrong. We assume there was a plan for man's brain, that the brain was created intentionally rather than accidentally or that the brain evolved with an intelligent purpose. So what would be the function, purpose, and reason for this half of man's brain?

If the right brain doesn't know fact from fiction, why would God give us a right brain? If the right brain cannot distinguish between right and wrong, what is the value of the right brain's logic? We have to believe that the right brain has a purpose; otherwise fully half of our brain is wasted.

We must recognize that when two things are equal but opposite they are also intrinsically connected. They are two different sides of the same thing. I believe that the right brain doesn't know right from wrong for a reason: so you won't be handcuffed by what you think you know, so you won't be handcuffed by what you have been taught by authority figures.

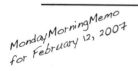
Be For What Is

My friend Brett Feinstein occasionally quotes his business partner, Jamie, as saying, "Be for what is." I think I understand what Jamie is saying.

There are basically two ways of seeing:
1. the way things ought to be.
2. the way things are.

Do you find yourself moaning about the injustice of it all and wishing that things were different? Follow the advice of Jamie and Bigteeth Teddy Roosevelt, who said, "Do what you can, with what you have, where you are."

Be for what is.

I wrote about this in chapter 76 of my first book, *The Wizard of Ads.* "Weasels are everywhere, incessantly singing their sad little song: If Only. 'If only I had a better education.' 'If only my boss liked me better.' 'If only I had married someone else.' 'If only I had invested in Chrysler when it was fifty cents a share...' There's a little weasel in all of us, and that weasel needs to be slapped. When your ears hear your lips start to sing the Song of the Weasel, you must learn to immediately slap the weasel within."

Now that we've established the wisdom of a pragmatic, clear-eyed worldview, let's examine the equal-but-opposite wisdom offered by that other hemisphere of your brain, the right. What might happen if a person simply rejected the way things are and insisted on seeing them as they ought to be?

1. First, the person would be considered irrelevant, an impractical dreamer.
2. If persistent, they'd become a nuisance.
3. Then a renegade, a rebel, a lunatic and a heretic.
4. Finally, a serious troublemaker and a borderline criminal.
5. Later, the founder of a movement.

Thomas Jefferson and George Washington.
Mahatma Gandhi. Martin Luther King.

"Every man with a new idea is a crank until the idea succeeds."
- Mark Twain

16

"The reasonable man adapts himself to the world; the unreasonable one persists in trying to adapt the world to himself. Therefore all progress depends upon the unreasonable man."

- George Bernard Shaw

I'm not trying to be mysterious when I say I agree with both of these equal-but-opposite worldviews. We must Be for What Is if we are to accomplish anything in the short term, and we must Be the Crank with a New Idea if tomorrow is going to be better than today.

Wizard Academy is a school for cranks with new ideas. Our plan is to change the world, one perspective at a time. I really can't put it more plainly than that. Is there anything in your world that needs changing? Come to Austin and we'll talk about it.

It was my favorite pioneering educational genius from Brazil, Paolo Freire, who said, "Education either functions as
1. an instrument which is used to facilitate integration of the younger generation into the logic of the present system and bring about conformity, or
2. it becomes the practice of freedom, the means by which men and women deal critically and creatively with reality and discover how to participate in the transformation of their world."

Paolo Freire would have liked Wizard Academy. Helen Keller would have been at home here, too. She said, "The heresy of one age becomes the orthodoxy of the next."

Wizard Academy alumni are the creators of tomorrow's orthodoxy in the sciences, the arts, and marketing. I believe Pablo Picasso would have loved it here. "I am always doing that which I cannot do, in order that I may learn how to do it."

You gotta love the Pablo.

But I think Robert Frost may have said it best:
"Most of the change we think we see in life
is due to truths being in and out of favor."

Like me, Frost realized that both perspectives are true. Our society simply moves from one extreme to the other in an arc spanning exactly 40 years. And we've been doing it since the beginning of time.

Roy H. Williams

Embrace Reckless Abandon

If we're not going to be bound by yesterday's knowledge, if we are to move beyond previously established knowledge and step out of the figurative box, we have to escape. We have to escape from the fear of shame and go to a place that doesn't know right from wrong, doesn't know fact from fiction, and truly doesn't care. We have to go to the place in our brain that has no concept of the fact that something could be immoral, unethical, wrong, illegal, shameful, or in any way impossible. This rejection of impossibility is feasible because *there is no place for impossibility* in the right hemisphere of our brain.

There has to be a place in our brain to say, "Yes, I see that this is incorrect. However, I need to move beyond the fact that this is incorrect in order to see that perhaps at another level, this idea is perfectly correct." This place in our brain must be able to identify and then move beyond the duality of a problem. The left brain can't do that. The left brain cannot ignore fact; nor can it ignore experience and authority. All of these things are vitally important to the left brain and cannot be dismissed.

If you believe that the only way to learn is through advice and example from an authority figure, that's classical classroom learning – a classical left brain download of pre-digested, pre-formatted information. But if we're only able to use what we already know, we'll never be able to move beyond our current level of knowledge.

You have to have a vehicle of absurdity, a vehicle of play, a vehicle that says, "I don't care and it doesn't matter. If this is ridiculous, that's good," if you are ever going to see what has not been seen before. You have to be able to escape the concrete rules of reality. When you need to think of new things, you have to be able to escape the fear of judgment by your peers, coworkers, boss, neighbors, friends, and society. You must be able to push those influences out of your head. Luckily, the right brain has no shame and no concept of ethics, judgment, or accuracy. The right brain is not married to right and wrong and it doesn't care.

Free the Beagle

In Roy H. William's book *Free the Beagle,* he asks readers to imagine that their left brain is a lawyer and their right brain is the lawyer's pet beagle. The beagle runs over and drops something at the feet of the lawyer. The lawyer says, "I don't have time to play right now. Leave me alone. I'm trying to concentrate." But the beagle was bringing the lawyer a clue to help him with his work. The beagle brought the lawyer a valuable treasure, but the beagle cannot speak and explain his gift. Unfortunately, the lawyer doesn't realize the significance of the beagle's gift. He thinks that his intellect is enough to solve the problem and disregards the beagle's assistance.

The left brain thinks like the lawyer. The left brain has an ego. Don't ever let anyone convince you that the left brain is enough alone, though, because if that is true, half of your brain exists for no reason at all – half of your brain is wasted.

In our society, how much time do you think adults spend *predominantly* in the right half of their brains during their conscious waking hours? We are never only in one side of the brain as opposed to the other; we're always in both. I believe that most of the time we're predominantly in our left brain with our right brain supporting. What few things do we do in our society as adults that would qualify as mostly right brain activities?

Watching a movie or reading a fiction book is a right-brain activity. Most movies are absolute fantasy fiction. A willing suspension of disbelief is required to enjoy these pursuits. We delve into the right hemisphere of our brain in order to escape the judgmental, analytical taskmaster of the left brain.

Bohr, a widely respected, hard-core scientist, understood that you have to have an outlet of ridiculousness to stimulate your right brain so that you are no longer limited by what is known to be possible. He understood that there was sometimes truth in the opposite of a "correct" statement. In order to be able to escape the left brain's absolute reverence of right and wrong, you have to be able to truly play. Unfortunately, true play is not as easily achieved as one might think.

For an activity to be play, the activity must be intrinsically motivating. If you play because you want to win a trophy, you're not really playing for pleasure and therefore not really playing. Play must also be freely chosen. If you're playing because someone told you to, you are not truly playing. Play must be actively engaging. You have to develop the willingness to say yes to the absurd, to the impulse, and you must have fun. You must derive pleasure from your play.

Ninety percent of the books written each year are nonfiction, but 90% of the books *purchased* each year are fiction.[1] That is a mind-boggling statistic. We think that people want facts, but the reality is that people want to escape from facts. People want to play and have the child inside of them unleashed.

Kurt Vonnegut once said, "I tell you, we are here on Earth to fart around, and don't let anybody tell you any different."

Freedom is actually a bigger game than power. Power is about what you can control, but freedom is about what you can unleash. Which entity do you think is bigger – that which you can control or that which is beyond our control and recognition?

---

[1] Wizard Academy Press

2008: Year of the Beagle

Courage... Curiosity... Intuition.

In the biggest news since Tiger Woods won the U.S. Open a beagle has taken top honors at Westminster for the first time in history. *Arooo! Aroo-Aroooooo!*

In the happy little village where I spend a lot of time, beagles are the symbol of curiosity and intuition, reliable guides to success in 2008.

Haven't you heard? Maintaining the status quo will yield a decline in 2008 for most business categories.

The February 8, 2008, issue of the *Wall Street Journal* had this to say:

> "Retailers turned in their worst monthly sales results in nearly five years, and big chains appeared to be girding themselves for a prolonged slowdown in consumer spending by announcing plans to close hundreds of stores and cut thousands of jobs."

> "Even gift-card redemptions, which were expected to give January sales figures a bigger lift, instead offered a glimpse at just how strapped consumers are. Wal-Mart Stores Inc. yesterday noted that redemptions were below its expectations, and said consumers were holding onto the cards longer -- or using them to buy groceries rather than treats like electronics."

The beagle called Intuition might seem to be a chaser of rabbits, rowdy without decorum, a runaway balloon on a windy day, but the joy of the beagle is neither random nor reckless. Her path connects the dots of an image too big to see, a pattern you'll recognize when you've climbed higher than where you stand.

Do you want to climb higher? Follow your beagle. She'll lead you to success.

2008 will be a grand adventure if you'll raise an intuitive ear and listen to what's blowing on the wind.

Roy H. Williams

Unleashing our Inner Wizard

At Wizard Academy, we celebrate outsider thinking and the wisdom of absurdity and audacity. We celebrate the weirdos, renegades, and mavericks – those that understand the importance of "thinking outside the box." In fact, these very traits are a defining characteristic of the people who are attracted to Wizard Academy.

Unfortunately, our wisdom is not universally celebrated. This type of thinking tends to be marginalized by society. We are in danger of *remaining* irrelevant to the rest of society if we don't come up with an analytical, logical, sequential, left-brain way of explaining these ideas and making them accessible to others. We don't want people to say, "Well, I'm not like you. I'm not fun loving and free and uninhibited and I don't get it. And you're just weird."

Their criticism isn't what worries us because we've lived with that kind of stereotyping our whole life. What worries us is that society will continue to ignore our ideas simply because they can't understand. The aim of this book is to take these right-brain concepts and explain them in a way that everyone can comprehend. We want to teach people what creative people do unconsciously so that they can make a conscious effort to produce similar results.

But first, you must fully recognize the duality and interconnectedness of the human brain. To escape the knowledge of what can't be done requires that you go into your right brain. So now, we're going to address some silly things.

Part 1 – The Basics

1
Lenny, Hank, Buck, and Walt

"Imagination is the one weapon in the war against reality."
Jules De Gaultier

*C*aterina dumps baby Lenny on her boyfriend then moves to town and gets married to someone else. Neither Lenny's father nor his mother is willing to give Lenny their family name, so he is known only by the name of the mountain under whose shadow he was born: Lenny Albano.

An unwanted child, Lenny grows up strangely in this remote rural neighborhood without access to comic books or video games. Estranged parents, odd relationships, a badly broken situation. But his imagination is intact. Is your imagination intact?

Long walks in the hills surrounding Mt. Albano cause Lenny to fall in love with animals. He loves them so much that he buys caged creatures just so that he can set them free. How Lenny makes his money is unimportant, but how he spends it reveals his soul. How do you spend your money?

People laugh when Lenny becomes a vegetarian, but he doesn't care. People have laughed at him since the day he was born. Lenny hides from them by taking journeys in his mind. He goes exploring deep inside his own head. Lenny is amazed by the things he finds. Lenny scribbles his thoughts in journals and draws little pictures in their margins. Although no publisher is willing to publish these random thoughts, Bill Gates recently paid $30 million for just one of Lenny's journals.

Lenny is very smart. But Lenny's deep curiosity causes him to be easily distracted. Although lots of people are willing to buy his paintings, rarely can he stay focused long enough to finish one. Lenny isn't completely alone in his quirky curiosity. When Lenny is 40, a man named Chris sails West to look for the East.

Go figure.

Long after Lenny dies, the world realizes how far ahead of time he had been. Sigmund Freud said Lenny was like a man who awoke too early in the darkness while the others were all still asleep. But we no longer call him by the name of the mountain under whose shadow he was born. We choose instead to call him by the name of the village he was from. And for some strange reason we insist on calling Lenny of Vinci, Leonardo. I think Lenny would have laughed had he known. And I think he would have fit right in at Wizard Academy.

Would you like to learn to see the world as Lenny did? In this section we'll look at the world through the eyes of Leonardo da Vinci, Genrikh Altshuller, Buckminster Fuller, and Walt Disney: the giants of innovation and creativity who rocked the world as we knew it.

Lenny (April 15, 1452 – May 2, 1519)

Infinitely curious and inventive, Leonardo da Vinci was a polymath: an architect, anatomist, sculptor, engineer, inventor, geometer, futurist, and painter. In fact, da Vinci is considered to be one of the greatest painters who ever lived, famous for his realistic paintings, such as the *Mona Lisa* and *The Last Supper*, as well as for influential drawings such as the *Vitruvian Man*.

Leonardo conceived visions of things vastly ahead of his time. The helicopter, tank, calculator, double hull ships, theory of plate tectonics, and the use of concentrated solar power were conceptualized by Leonardo, although very few of his designs were constructed or even feasible during his lifetime. Although da Vinci greatly advanced our knowledge in the fields of anatomy, astronomy, civil engineering, optics, and hydrodynamics (the study of water), modern science was only in its infancy when Lenny was alive and the greatness of his ideas was not recognized. As Freud said, Lenny was like a man who awoke too early in the darkness while the others were all still asleep.

Lenny's approach to science was that of a curious observer. Rather than examining his observations and discoveries through the lens of experiments or explanation, da Vinci simply tried to understand the world by describing and depicting each phenomenon as he saw it. If he had been hung up on the details or been driven by a need to prove or disprove his observations, he would never have been able to contribute such a vast array of knowledge to the world.

The legendary curiosity of Leonardo da Vinci was horizontal, not vertical. He never studied narrow and deep. Lenny looked for the pattern – the connectedness of things.

Hank (October 15, 1926 – September 24, 1998)

Genrikh Altshuller was a Russian engineer, scientist, journalist, and writer. In his book, *And Suddenly the Inventor Appeared*, Altschuller said, "I got my first patent while in the tenth grade. Later there were other inventions. I worked at the patent office and had meetings with different inventors. I became more and more interested in the mechanics of creativity. How were inventions made? What happens in the head of the inventor?" Altshuller believed that it was possible for people to "learn" to become inventors.

While working on a commission on innovation for the Russian Navy, Altshuller embarked on a mission to prove his theory and establish a set of generic rules to explain the conception of new patentable ideas. Altshuller studied hundreds of thousands of patents, only to discover that there are only about 1,500 basic problems. Incredibly, he also found that each of these problems could be solved by applying one or more of the 40 universal answers.

That's right. *Every* answer to *every* problem is found within the 40 principles of TRIZ (pronounced trees), the Theory of Inventive Problem Solving.

Altshuller's curiosity led him to question the "learnability" of creativity. In *Creativity as an Exact Science*, he said, "Although people who had achieved a great deal in science and technology talked of the inscrutability of creativity, I was not convinced and disbelieved them immediately and without argument. Why should everything but creativity be open to scrutiny? What kind of process can this be which unlike all others is not subject to control? ... what can be more alluring than the discovery of the nature of talented thought and converting this thinking from occasional and fleeting flashes into a powerful and controllable fire of knowledge?"

Altshuller's personal creativity was devoted to understanding creativity and innovation in others. His original intention for the creation of TRIZ was to solve engineering and design issues; however, the principles of TRIZ are now being successfully applied to both social issues and business dilemmas. Today TRIZ is a set of tools – a model-based technology for generating innovative ideas and solutions. Altshuller's work has made TRIZ both teachable and learnable. In short, Altshuller's ideas have made it possible for *anyone* to learn to become a systematic, creative thinker.

Buck (July 12, 1895 – July 1, 1983)

In 1927, at the age of 32, Buckminster Fuller stood on the shores of Lake Michigan, prepared to throw himself into the freezing waters and end his life. His first child had died. He was bankrupt, discredited and jobless, and he had a wife and newborn daughter. Standing on the shore on the verge of suicide, Buck was suddenly struck by the thought that his life belonged, not to himself, but to the universe.

At that moment, Buckminster Fuller chose to embark on what he called "an experiment to discover what the little, penniless, unknown individual might be able to do effectively on behalf of all humanity." Over the course of the next 54 years, he proved time and again that his most controversial ideas were both practical and workable. During the course of this remarkable experiment, Fuller[2]

- was awarded 28 U.S. patents
- wrote 28 books
- received 47 honorary doctorates in the arts, science, engineering, and the humanities
- created work which was gathered into the permanent collections of museums around the globe
- received dozens of major architectural and design awards including the Gold Medal of the American Institute of Architects and the Gold Medal of the Royal Institute of British Architects
- circled the globe 57 times, reaching millions through his public lectures and interviews

---

[2] Buckminster Fuller Institute. www.bfi.org. Accessed 22 Feb. 2008.

Buckminster Fuller was another man who lived before his time. He devoted his life to answering the question, "Does humanity have a chance to survive lastingly and successfully on planet Earth, and if so, how?" As a practical philosopher, he viewed his ideas as "artifacts." Some of these inventions were built as prototypes, while others still exist only on paper. Regardless of their current status, Fuller believed each of his creations were technically viable.

Fuller is best known for the creation of the geodesic dome – the lightest, strongest, and most cost-effective structure ever invented. His domes are able to cover more space without internal supports than any other enclosure. The domes become proportionally lighter and stronger as they grow in size. The geodesic dome is viewed today as a breakthrough in architectural design due to its cost-effectiveness and ease of construction. Today, more than 300,000 of Fuller's domes have been built around the world.

Walt (December 5, 1901 – December 15, 1966)

Walter Elias Disney is known as one of the most influential and innovative figures in the 20th century entertainment industry. Disney was a master of visual and spatial intelligence. His unique ability to see the "big picture" without the hindrance of boundaries, limitations, or restraint, enabled him to provide the public with what they desired. Disney's creative capabilities have been compared to those of Albert Einstein, in part because of both men's use of highly *visual* and *physical* fantasies in their discoveries.

Walt Disney's creativity was twofold. Disney possessed the capability to uncover new relationships between concepts and look at subjects from an entirely new view point. Disney looked at the *connectedness* of things, and was able to create new combinations using existing elements. This creativity enabled Disney to imagine new technologies that paved the way to improved business processes. One of Disney's greatest innovations was the development of the story board. The story board, or visual depiction of Disney's fantasies, allowed him to document and communicate "the big picture" behind his big ideas.

Disney's physical fantasies also came to fruition. Like the other great minds we've examined in this chapter, Disney was concerned with the obstacles standing in the way of human creativity.

EPCOT, the Experimental Prototype Community of Tomorrow, was designed as a live showcase for the creativity of American industry. Disney said, "I don't believe there is a challenge anywhere in the world that is more important to people everywhere than finding the solutions to the problems of our cities. But where do we begin? Well, we're convinced we must start with public need. And the need is not just for curing the old ills of old cities. We think the need is for starting from scratch on virgin land and building a community that will become a prototype for the future."

Great Minds Think Alike

All of these great men were seen as misfits, but in all actuality they were creative geniuses. In my opinion, Lenny, Hank, Buck, and Walt all used the same fundamentals of creativity and innovation, even as the processes they used varied.

Although these innovators could not have been conscious of their common link, I believe their thought processes are evidence of their mutual greatness.

Was Leonardo da Vinci instinctively using the 40 Answers of Genrikh Altshuller's TRIZ? In the coming chapters, we'll discuss the "basics" of these four men's creative thought processes and examine how these principles align with the "tactics" of TRIZ.

I believe these men, as well as most creative minds, used these basics either consciously or unconsciously. I have named these basics: "Peel the Onion," "Try It," "Sensible Design," "Clear as Mud," "View Point," and "Universal Network," in addition to the TRIZ fundamental "Ideal Final Result."

As these great thinkers have proved, creativity and innovation *can* be taught.

Would you like to learn?

2
Peel the Onion

"A man should live if only to satisfy his curiosity."
Yiddish Proverb

"Well, they are more hot-dog shaped than normal."

The shape was the only thing I had noticed that might be different. Truthfully, I was afraid to say anything at all, but after a long pause that seemed to span hours of time, I knew my boss was waiting for someone to throw out an idea. I also knew from experience that we weren't leaving that room until we had come up with some new theories.

"*What* is more hot-dog shaped?" Joe Lombardo, the general manager of Thiokol Corporation, demanded.

"The AP particles," I replied. "AP particles are never perfectly round. They are more elongated like an ellipse of sorts, but this batch looks more stretched out than normal, more like a hot dog."

Ammonium Percholorate (AP) is a major ingredient in the fuel used by Space Shuttle Solid Rocket Boosters. AP is a finely ground powder that could be mistaken for flour if you didn't know any better.

The burn rate of this particular batch of propellant was, well ... acting funny. We had been over the specifications for the raw materials and everything was "nominal," as rocket scientists often say, at least relative to the specifications.

"Is the *shape* within specs?" Joe asked.

"Well, yes and no. The spec only covers particle size. It doesn't say anything about shape."

"Really? Well, let's peel this onion back a little further. Does the particle shape affect the burn characteristics?"

"I don't know, but you would probably think so."

"Then why does the spec not cover shape?"

"I don't know. I didn't write it. That was before my time."

"OK, then let's peel the onion back another layer and go find out."

Joe Lombardo had several signature phrases he used to encourage curiosity and critical thought. "Peel the onion," was one of his favorites. "Let's shake hands with the physics," was another. He wanted his team to remain curious at all times in order to get to the bottom of what was going on.

Fortunately, I was curious enough myself to want to know why the propellant was acting funny before the meeting. I didn't have any idea what I would find, but once everything was found to be within spec, I decided to look at the AP under a microscope, even though this step was not required. I compared what I saw under the scope to earlier data. Although I could not pinpoint the difference exactly, in general this funny batch seemed more hot-dog like.

We learned through a subsequent investigation that the shape did have an effect on the propellant burn rate. We got a lot smarter by peeling the layers of the onion and always asking "why" (or why not).

Everything You Know is Wrong

This kind of curious attitude makes innovation and discoveries possible. Too many people rely on conventional wisdom as the *primary* source of knowledge and information. The problem with conventional wisdom is twofold. As we discussed in the introduction, if you're starting with what is known and you're only willing to look at what can be extrapolated from the known, then how do you discover a thing that is not directly relative to the known? Furthermore:

Conventional wisdom is wrong 100% of the time…..

in some context or percentage.

If that statement shocks you, perhaps you will find Roy's summation of my statement easier to digest. "Conventional wisdom at its best is still incomplete."

Sadly, conventional wisdom kills curiosity – and without curiosity there can be no creativity. So let's get curious for a moment.

Middle School Science Class

Every person who has been through the U.S. or Canadian school system has studied the solar radiometer at some point in their education. The solar radiometer was designed by William Crooks in 1873.

You know how a solar radiometer works, right? When the sunlight shines on the dome, the paddles spin. The more intense the sunlight is, the faster the paddles spin. But how does a solar radiometer really work? Do you remember?

Despite what you might have learned in school, we actually have **no idea**. *Nobody in the world knows how the solar radiometer works.*

Below are some common theories as to how the radiometer works. Beneath each theory, you'll find the reason why that theory must be incorrect.

- Radiation Pressure
    - The photon pressure is too weak to move the vanes.
- Gas Pressure
    - The air is warmer on the black side.
    - Why would it hit the black side anymore than anything else?
- Outgassing of Black Material
    - The radiometer would quit working when the gas is gone, but it doesn't.
- Photoelectric Effect
    - The radiometer works with material that has no photoelectric properties
- Convection Currents
    - Why would the vanes blow in a single direction?

We take all of these reasons why the radiometer works for granted, but in reality, none of these theories are accurate. Regardless of the fact that all of these teachings are incorrect, school teachers continue to perpetuate the "conventional wisdom" behind the workings of this machine. The way a radiometer works is just one of thousands and thousands of things that we are taught that just is not true.

We have no idea how a solar radiometer works, yet we continue to teach our students inaccurate theories. What do you think that does to their curiosity?

You Swine

The principles in this book do not apply exclusively to technical or scientific issues. These principles apply to all aspects of your business and personal life.

I used "Peel the Onion" a couple of years ago with one of my clients. She sells pigs for a living – not exactly rocket science.

"So what issues do you want to work on today in our creative thinking workshop?"

"We need more sales!"
(Never heard that one before)

"Why do you think sales are not growing like you want them to?"

"I don't know. It doesn't make sense."

"Does your competition provide a better product or service?"

"No, in fact even our *competition* will admit we have the best bloodline and breed of pigs on the market. All of the review magazines rate us number one; in fact, we have the highest customer retention rate in the business: 98%. The 2% of customers that actually leave us leave because they got out of the pig business all together or the owner died!" (FYI – yes, there are pig review magazines out there.)

"Well let's peel this onion back a little. If you have the best product on the market what is stopping you from getting more market share?"

"Customers just don't want to switch providers even when they know we can offer them something better."

"Why?" (keep peeling)

"Well it is the risk of switching to us. The average herd is about a $250,000 investment and they feel the risk in switching is too great. If they switched to us and our herd acquired a disease or something the loss could financially ruin them. They can't afford that kind of loss."

"Does this ever happen with your pigs?"

"No never. We have the best breed on the market."

"Never? Really? Never?"

"No. Never."

"Then why don't you eliminate the risk for them? Put your money where your mouth is. If you are so confident that your product is superior and that there is literally no, or at least a very remote risk of illness, why don't you guarantee potential customers that you will pay the $250,000 if anything happens. Promise to replace their herd with the herd of their choice if they get sick."

"No one in the industry offers anything that radical."

"Why not be the first and dramatically differentiate yourself then?"

To their credit, and my joy, they implemented this policy. They are quickly gaining market share. I don't mention the company name at their request; they want to turn the industry on its head before the competition knows what hit them.

Time Travel

We view time travel as a science fiction fantasy, but has time travel been proven? Think about that question from a curious point of view. I'm not asking if time travel is possible, but rather whether or not the theory of time travel has been proven.

Although this may come as a surprise to some, time travel has been proven thousands of times. In fact, time travel is proven every single day. Einstein's Theory of Relativity says that the faster an object goes, the slower time goes relative to that object. When you approach the speed of light, time will stop for the observer.

Scientists can watch a particle degrade in a particle accelerator. They watch this occurrence thousands of times, and they know exactly how long it takes each particle to degrade. However, when you fly a particle in a particle accelerator past an observer at a speed near the speed of light, the particle takes ten, a hundred, or a thousand times longer to degrade. How can that be possible unless time was slowing down for the observer?

The Global Positioning System (GPS) is essentially a bunch of clocks on satellites. GPS receivers pick up signals from the satellites and determine your position by measuring how long the radio signal took to get to your receiver and bounce back. GPS systems use geometry and triangulation to determine the distance.

When the GPS system was being designed, someone raised the question, "What if Einstein's theory was right?" The satellites fly around at different speeds and different distances from an observer on the ground. If Einstein was in fact correct, then the clocks would have all shown different times and the whole system would be worthless. As a result of this conversation, there was a big debate about the extra cost of upgrading the satellite system to update the clocks continuously based on the orbit changes and speeds.

Guess what? Einstein was exactly right. Fortunately, they ultimately decided to spend the extra money to upgrade the

GPS clocks. GPS clocks are updated continuously, every day, by a United States Air Force team known as the 2nd Space Operations Squadron (2 SOPS)[3].

Time travel has been proven many, many times. Conventional wisdom was once again … wrong.

By the way, do you think Alzheimer's is a form of time travel?

Are you sure?

Space Shuttle Challenger

At times, creativity doesn't require any more than some plain old common sense and a little curiosity. On January 28th, 1986, the Space Shuttle Challenger exploded during launch. The cause of the catastrophe was eventually revealed to be the Solid Rocket Booster (SRB) O-rings.

It was widely reported that the O-rings failed due to the cold temperatures at the launch, but could the weather alone really have caused the accident?

At the time of launch it was 36°F outside, but the outside surface temperature of the SRBs was, on average, 12°F. How in the world could the SRBs be 12°F when the temperature outside was 36°F?

Most people ignore this discrepancy. I suppose they assume the difference was due to "wind chill." Wind chill, however, is a phenomenon that only people and living things can experience.

[3] 2D Space Operations Squadron. http://en.wikipedia.org/wiki/2d_Space_Operations_ Squadron. Accessed 23 Feb. 2008.

Wind chill does not relate to actual temperature. Wind chill is the sensation you get when cold air blows across your skin and removes some of the heat your body has produced. All wind chill does is makes you *feel* colder. But for something that is not alive, like the Space Shuttle, there is no such thing as wind chill.

So you have this 36°F wind blowing past the SRBs, yet the SRBs are only 12°F. Now 36°F sounds cold to you and me, but that's a warm temperature compared to 12°F. This 36°F wind should have heated the SRB to 36°F as well, but it didn't.

The SRBs couldn't possibly have stayed at 12°F unless something was *keeping* them that cold: something that has nothing to do with the weather. This mysterious coolant would have to be something really, really, cold to keep the SRBs at 12°F with all that hot air blowing past them.

Consider this real-life application. You're at the beach with a cooler full of beer on a warm summer day. The beer is chilled to perfection. You pop open a beer and stick the can in the dirt. What do you think is going to happen? Well, you *know* what's going to happen. The beer is going to get warm. The beer can't stay cold unless something is keeping it cold.

The only thing on the launch pad that I know of that has that kind of cooling power was the liquid hydrogen (423°F below zero) and liquid oxygen (297°F below zero) in the external tank.

In the 1980s the External Tank (ET) experienced periodic problems with cracks and leaks. Could the liquid hydrogen and/or liquid oxygen have been leaking on the SRBs?

If you don't think so, then what is your explanation for the SRBs being 12°F? For the record, the temperature never dropped that low during the night either. Furthermore, the vent at the top of the ET is 150 feet away, so the vent couldn't have reached the bottom of the SRBs, either. Aren't you curious why the SRBs were 12°F?

The presidential report makes no mention nor offers any explanation of how the SRBs could be 12°F when it was a balmy 36°F outside. And it's not like there weren't a lot of smart people looking at this; Neil Armstrong, Richard Feynman, Sally Ride, and Chuck Yeager were all part of the investigation team. Did everyone miss this discrepancy? Why were more people not more curious about this puzzling temperature differentiation?

Why didn't more people "Peel the Onion" and try to resolve the temperature discrepancy?

Note to readers: Yes, I know this is a controversial subject and, no, I am not against the Space Program. I had the honor and privilege to work on the Space Shuttle for 15 years. That position was the highlight of my career.

By the way, I was at the launch pad on January 28, 1986.

Curiosity Killed ...

If you thought I was going to say the cat, you couldn't be more wrong. I hate that saying. Curiosity hasn't killed anything – in fact, curiosity itself is killed by conventional wisdom.

Think about tuna fish for a moment. Why was tuna sold in the exact same form, fit, and function "can" for almost 100 years? For a long time, tuna was just tuna. There wasn't any oil or albacore, or anything fancy – just tuna. There was no lemon-flavored, light, herb seasoned tuna, nor was tuna sold in soft packaging. Why is that? All those possibilities existed for those 100 years. Mostly because people didn't stop to question why. No one stopped and asked themselves, "What else can we do?"

Challenging conventional wisdom and being curious is one of the most important things I've ever done. I constantly challenge wisdom and authority for two reasons. One, because challenging wisdom and authority is fun, and two, because most people have no idea what they're talking about. When I present classes to major organizations, someone always interrupts me to say, "We can't do that here. That's against our policies and/or regulations."

When someone says that, I stop. I say, "OK. By a show of hands, tell me how many of you have actually read the regulation?"

I'll usually get one or two brave souls who will put their hands in the air. Then I say, "OK, you read them. But did you challenge the interpretation of the regulations? Because there's a very good chance that when the regulations were written their intentions may have been something altogether different. I'll bet you that the original intent of the regulation and your interpretation are not the same."

And the people drop their hands. Conventional wisdom kills curiosity because someone always steps in and says, "You can't do it that way," or "We already know how that works so why are you still talking about it?!"

What Do I Know? I'm Just a Doctor!

My doctor's real name isn't Becker, but the role played by Ted Danson in the popular sitcom proves a remarkable likeness in personality.

One day, I was sitting in my doctor's office anxiously waiting to hear the results of my most recent cholesterol screening. The previous year my cholesterol had gone up just slightly, which was very depressing. I essentially had no exercise regiment prior to that, but afterward I went into fat-free mode and started walking 4 miles a day. In spite of my protests, a couple of years earlier my doctor had put me on a low dose of blood pressure medication. I don't even like to take aspirin.

As a result of my hard work, I was certain my current cholesterol level would be outstanding. I couldn't wait to hear the great results.

Unfortunately, the test results painted a different picture. My cholesterol level was 30 points higher.

"That's impossible. I don't eat beef brisket anymore... ever! I don't eat any sausage, never go to McDonalds, buy fat-free everything, and walk 4 miles a day. It can't be true."

"Yeah, it sucks getting old doesn't it? Aging is that one thing you can't control. Even though you're trying to eat better and exercising, which is a great thing, these efforts are obviously not enough."

"What? Older? It has only been a year! Urrrrrrr...this doesn't make any sense. It's not fair."

"I think we should put you on Lipitor."

"No. I don't want to take anymore meds. Let me think about it for a while. This makes no sense."

When something makes no sense to you, your curiosity needs to kick into high gear. Well, this surely qualified as nuts to me. Yes, I was a year older, but... come on. The test results couldn't be right. Most people would probably just do as the doctor ordered, but I almost never take anything at face value.

So I racked my brain for days. What else could be causing this spike? What had changed in my life in the last one or two years? I was exercising more and eating better, but my cholesterol was going in the wrong direction. The only thing I could come up with was this: two years prior to the test I started taking a dietary supplement called glucosamine sulfate. I had read that this supplement helps with joints – elbows, ankles and knees – and as I had sprained my knee a few years ago snowshoeing, I thought that this nutrient might ease the pain I felt on walks.

So I went to the Internet to do some research. After some time, I found a page on the Arthritis Foundation's Web site that talked about glucosamine sulfate. At the end of the article it said:

"Yes, glucosamine sulfate can help lubricate your joints and make them feel better, but be careful and watch your triglycerides, glucosamine sulfate is made from shellfish and has been known to elevate cholesterol in some people."

Aha! I'd found the smoking gun.

I went back to Becker to explain my discovery.

"I found this information about glucosamine sulfate on the Internet...," I began.

"Don't believe anything you read on the Web, they are nothing but a bunch of kooks."

So I handed him the printout of the article with the Arthritis Foundation logo prominently displayed at the top of the page.

"This is some research I found from the Arthritis Foundation."

"Oh ... well they are a pretty reputable organization."

Thirty seconds of complete radio silence.

"Well, what the hell do I know? I'm just your doctor. Get off the crap for 2 months and come back and we will check your levels again."

So I did. Two months later, my cholesterol was 30 points lower and back under the limit.

If I did not have a curious nature about most everything I would have been on another needless medication. It pays to peel the onion back.

Spark Your Own Curiosity

I recently had an argument with my wife about cell phones and driving. I believed that women talked on cell phones while driving more than men. She didn't agree. So, I got curious.

I sat in my driveway for several hours and counted how many men and women I saw drive by on their phones. I took a 1,000 car sample, and what do you know? The numbers came out even. Even though I proved my own wisdom wrong, I'm proud to say that I questioned myself. I got curious and took action to find out whether or not I was right.

One of the biggest things I've done for my career is to schedule learning time. Ever since I was 20 years old, I've scheduled two, two-hour sessions each week to do nothing but think and try something new. I also spend one day of each month doing the same thing. I read a trade journal from an industry I know nothing about, or I go to the junk yard. Last year, I actually went to kindergarten for a day. I've even read a couple of chapters in a Danielle Steele book (I almost threw up, no wait … honestly I did throw up) – just to make me think about something in a different way.

How many people do you know that actually do that? How many people actually schedule time to think about new things and learn? Quite frankly, not enough.

What outside people, places, activities, and situations do *you* use to stimulate your thinking? What do you do when you're facing a mental block on an issue? The next time you have a problem, ask for help. Just don't ask the "expert."

The expert is probably not the best person to approach to find new ideas. An expert is the authority on a subject because they are well versed in conventional wisdom. Specialization is a fact of life, but specialization also limits creativity. There is a great need for cross-fertilization to generate new ideas.

Rather than asking the expert, purposefully pick someone in a different industry or department to talk to. If you're ever in need of a new sounding board, go to score.org. This Web site is run by a bunch of retired CEOs and executives who have nothing to do but give you their advice (for free!). On the drop-down menu of industries, select someone in a field that has nothing to do with your problem. If you have a marketing question, pick an IT guy – and pray. Of course, you'll have to send your target an e-mail that explains why you've picked them; otherwise their first reaction will be "you've got the wrong guy." You've got to tell them that you don't have the wrong guy – that you picked them because you're looking for a new perspective. Try that out for some fresh ideas.

You can also take somebody that you really *hate* out to lunch. Yes ... someone you truly hate. Present the problem or issue that's been troubling you and then shut up for 15 minutes. You probably won't have an easy time keeping your mouth shut, but just try anyway. I promise they will say something that will make you think of something creative that you hadn't thought of before – and you might just find out that you don't actually hate the person.

Challenge yourself to do something new. Schedule a time each week to do something to spark your curiosity. You can even start small. Try taking a walk each morning and looking for 10 new things that you have never noticed before, even if you have walked that path 1,000 times. You'd be surprised by how much more you'll notice about your world when you look at it from a new perspective.

As Charlie "Tremendous" Jones once said, "The only difference between where you are now and where you'll be next year is the books you read and the people you meet."

In Alan Lightman's book, *A Sense of the Mysterious*, he says, "Not long ago, sitting at my desk at home, I suddenly had the *horrifying* realization that I no longer waste time."

Read both of these passages again.

Remember: 100% of the time, at least a part of conventional wisdom is wrong. If you never stop to question what you already know, if you never stop to indulge your curiosity, you'll never discover anything new.

Remain curious, just like our friend Lenny.

3
Try It

"I have not failed. I've found 10,000 ways that don't work."
Thomas Alva Edison

Most new discoveries don't result in a "eureka" moment, but rather a puzzled, "what the hell just happened?"

That ever-elusive eureka moment is the result of testing, experimenting, demonstrating, and asking questions. The end result is often unexpected, but once the unforeseen result has reared its head, the accidental inventor's *curiosity* will take over and ask, "Why?"

At that point, the inventor has to test and demonstrate to explain their unexpected results.

The Radar Range

In 1940, scientists Sir John Randall and Dr. H.A. Boot invented the magnetron, a key component of radar, in a lab at Birmingham University in England. Radar, which stands for Radio Detecting And Ranging, was used to bounce microwaves off enemy war crafts to detect their presence.[4]

In 1946, Dr. Percy Spencer accidentally stumbled upon an entirely new use for the magnetron. The engineer was running tests on a magnetron tube in his Raytheon Company lab when he was hit by a chocolate craving. Spencer reached into his pocket to retrieve the treat and realized that his chocolate bar had melted into a gooey mess.

Spencer knew that the magnetron produced heat, but he had

---

[4] Microwave Ovens. http://home.nycap.rr.com/useless/microwaves/index.html. Accessed 01 Mar. 2008.

not felt any of the heat waves during the test. He also suspected that the magnetron was responsible for the current state of his chocolate – after all, his body heat had never melted a bar before.

So, Spencer got curious. He decided to explore his accidental discovery further and ask "why?" He placed a bag of popcorn in front of the magnetron tube, and the popcorn popped all over the floor. The next day, he decided to try to cook an egg. Another scientist got a little too close and the egg blew up in his face – but the egg was in fact, cooked.

And so, Raytheon created the first microwave oven, known as the Radar Range.

The Pill Did What?!

In the 1990s, a group of pharmaceutical chemists at Pfizer's Sandwich, Kent research facility in England created a compound known as Sidenafil. Sidenafil was designed to treat hypertension (high blood pressure) and angina pectoris (a form of cardiovascular disease). Clinical trials revealed that although the drug did little to treat angina, there was one totally unexpected, yet remarkable side effect.[5]

Sidenafil induced penile erections.

Known today as Viagra, this little blue pill was approved for use as an erectile dysfunction aid by the FDA in March 1998. Viagra was the first pill on the market to treat E.D., and quickly became a runaway success. Between 1999 and 2001, annual sales of Viagra exceeded $1 billion!

Nobody in the world dreamed about Viagra's "side effect." I wish I had been able to be a part of that research team. On a paper survey of the drug's effects, how many people do you

---

[5] Sildenfil. http://en.wikipedia.org/wiki/Viagra. Accessed 29 Feb. 2008.

think were forthcoming about that unexpected result? Once the researchers discovered the drug's more popular (and marketable) use, they had to actually test and demonstrate the medication.

Fight Fire with Fire

Researchers believe that smallpox first surfaced in human civilization around 10,000 B.C.[6] Smallpox was an epidemic of epic proportions at the turn of the last millennium. During the 18th century alone, the disease killed an estimated 400,000 people each year, including five reigning European monarchs. Smallpox proved fatal in 20 to 60% of infection cases, with even more tragic results in children. Eighty percent of children infected with the disease died.

In 1796 a doctor in rural England took note of a peculiar thing. Dr. Edward Jenner noticed that milk maids who were infected with a skin disease known as cowpox appeared to be immune to smallpox.

Cowpox is related to the smallpox virus, but the disease is not really harmful to humans. Cowpox got its name from the manner in which the disease was transmitted; cow maids got the disease from touching the udders of infected cows.

Jenner was curious as to why the cowpox seemed to protect the milk maids from the deadly smallpox infection. He decided to find out why, and embarked on a mission to shed light on the mystery. Jenner's experiments revealed that smallpox immunity could be produced by injecting a person with material from a cowpox lesion. Sure enough, cowpox inoculations created smallpox immunity.

Jenner called the materials used in the inoculation a vaccine. Vaccine is derived from the root word *vacca*, which is Latin for cow.

---

[6] Smallpox. http://en.wikipedia.org/wiki/Smallpox. Accessed 03 Mar. 2008.

In the 19th century, the cowpox virus used for the vaccine was replaced by the vaccinia virus, an infection in the same family. Almost 200 years after Jenner's discovery, the World Health Organizations certified the eradication of the disease, in 1979.

Today, smallpox remains the only human infectious disease to have been successfully eradicated from nature.

Jenner's curiosity and subsequent testing saved countless lives, and helped rid the world of a dangerously infectious epidemic.

When Knowledge Isn't Enough

Looking to make a change? Remember: transformation happens experientially, not intellectually.

We often receive instruction and agree, "I see what you're saying," but seldom do we actually do the thing we learned. We just agree with it in our minds.

This is a problem.

Daniel J. Boorstin said, "The greatest obstacle to discovery is not ignorance – it is the illusion of knowledge."

Boorstin's statement becomes particularly poignant when you learn that he graduated with highest honors from Harvard, was a Rhodes Scholar at Oxford and earned his PhD at Yale. By occupation he was a lawyer, a university professor and the U.S. Librarian of Congress from 1975 to 1987. Yet Boorstin warned us that the illusion of knowledge was the greatest impediment to discovery.

Are you willing to go exploring with Boorstin and Dewar and Michener and me? Tommy Dewar said, "Exploration makes one wiser; even if the only wisdom gained is to know where not to return."

James Michener won the Pulitzer Prize in 1948 for his book, *Tales of the South Pacific.* He went on to earn more than **one hundred million dollars** as the author of more than 40 novels.

In his memoirs – published just a year before he died at the age of 90 – Michener wrote, "I feel almost a blood relationship with all the artists in all the mediums, for I find that we face the same problems but solve them in our own ways. When young people in my writing classes, for example, ask what subjects they should study to become writers, I surprise them by replying: 'Ceramics and eurhythmic dancing.' When they look surprised I explain: 'Ceramics so you can feel form evolving through your fingertips molding the moist clay, and eurhythmic dancing so you can experience the flow of motion through your body. You might develop a sense of freedom that way.'"

– *This Noble Land,* chap.10

Michener, a novelist to whose success George Washington testified one hundred million times, instructed thousands of aspiring young writers during his years at the University of Texas and he gave each student the same advice. But do you suppose any of them actually took classes in ceramics and eurhythmic dancing?

I doubt it.

Would you have done what Michener said? Or would you have thought, "I get it," and then walked on to seek advice from other experts?

Would you have allowed the illusion of knowledge to rob you of the joy of discovery?

Roy H. Williams

Just Do It

The next time you have an idea, go ahead and try it. Test your theory or idea.

Creativity is coming up with an idea; innovation is getting off your butt and doing something about it.

Roy Williams has told me many times that anyone can be a best-selling author. The recipe is this:

- Pick a topic you're interested in
- Think about the topic a lot
- Think about it some more
- Develop your own *unique theory* about what it all means
- Just do it – go out and test your theory
- Write a book about it

Roy has an African friend named Akintunde Omitowoju from Nigeria. After Akintunde heard Harry Nilsson's song "Coconut," he asked Roy if lime and coconut were really good together.

Roy realized that he, in fact, had never heard of anyone who actually tried to put de lime in de coconut, and so he said, "Akintunde, we're going to do this."

In the da Vinci course, Roy tells a story about the two of them sitting together in his living room, passing a coconut shell filled with their concoction back and forth.

According to Roy, coconut milk and lime juice actually make a pretty good combination – but he never would have had the opportunity to experience the drink if they hadn't actually created the concoction and tried it out.

How many people wonder why something is the way it is, but never stop to find out? How many people have a brilliant idea, and get excited about their idea, only to do nothing? Most people never take action to test their theory or try out their plan.

Curiosity is important, but you'll only see results if you actually take steps to test your hypothesis and answer the questions you've raised.

Fear of Failure

One of the key things to keep in mind when you are being creative and testing and demonstrating is to leave yourself *a lot* of room for error. You're always going to experience failures and make mistakes; that's just a fact of life.

Despite the necessity of failure to success, many people allow their fear of failure to prevent them from taking action.

Do you remember Ken Jennings? Ken holds the record for the longest winning streak on the show Jeopardy. He won 74 games before he was defeated, and earned an estimated $3,022,700 on the show.

In my opinion, Ken only made two mistakes in his life – well, at least in his life on Jeopardy. One was when he lost on purpose because they paid him to quit (that's my theory and I'm sticking to it). His other mistake came in the form of a truly awkward answer.

The question was Tool Time for $200.

Alex: This term for a long-handled gardening tool can also mean an immoral pleasure seeker.

Ken: What's a *hoe*?

The next time you make a mistake, put your error in perspective. At least you're not a clean-cut Mormon with 6 million people watching you say, "What's a hoe?" on national television (the answer was "What is a rake?"). Keep that in perspective.

Give Yourself Great Odds

Fear of failure stops many people in their tracks. I once had an angel investor approach me after a workshop. He said that he and his friends had a $30 million fund. They wanted to start a bunch of companies, and they needed smart people to help. My first reaction was, "I don't want to take anyone else's money and fail." That's what I kept thinking the whole time he was talking.

Later that night, we went out to dinner to discuss the subject further – and he said something that made me rethink everything.

"Here's what I think would be absolutely glaring success. We start 10 companies. Eight of them fail, one breaks even, and one makes me some money. If even one of them succeeds, that is *unbelievable* success."

Think about that for a moment. When I was told that I was allowed to fail, my perspective changed. I think I've got a pretty good chance of being successful, especially if I'm allowed to screw up 85% of the time.

After that conversation, I said, "Wow. OK, now I am interested. Let's talk some more."

You can give yourself good odds, too, by just being willing to try. Just do something for the sake of your own curiosity and don't worry about the end result. If you stop and think about it, failure and success is all perception anyway.

If you ever want to experience that eureka moment, if you ever want to taste great success, you have to be willing to try – and be willing to fail, so get off your keister and do something!

What Courage Can Do
With Six Dollars

Brad Lawrence has been a client of my firm for 12 years. During that time, he's grown his business beyond all expectations - mostly because he's got guts.

Recently, Brad was looking at a sort of charm bracelet for his jewelry store. He could buy the base bracelets for 6 dollars apiece if he ordered at least 500. That would be $3,000. But his real investment would be another $30,000 for the countless beads and charms with which women could personalize their bracelets.

His friends gave him lots of advice:

"Charm bracelets are dead. That trend has come and gone."

"They'll bring in the wrong customer. You'll lose your reputation for upscale sophistication."

"It would cost more to advertise the charm bracelets than you could make on them."

What did Brad decide? He decided to order 500 bracelets and give them all away.

My staff and I said, "Hurray!"

Here's what his friends said:

"People won't value the bracelet if they get it for free."

"People will take the bracelets, then sell them on eBay."

"Giving away jewelry will make you look desperate."

But Brad knew the story of K. C. Gillette, the man who gave away 90,884 razor handles in 1904 in the hope of selling disposable blades. By 1910 he was one of the richest men in America. Last year his company did more than $9 billion.

How did it work out for Brad?

The 500 free bracelets were gone in less than a week.
And within 6 weeks Brad had sold more than $100,000 worth of beads

and charms. Only 28 people who took a bracelet failed to buy any ornaments for it.

This week Brad told me, "Groups of women are coming into the store during their lunch hour to shop for ornaments, beads and charms. Every day is like a party. The traffic is amazing. We're making lots of new friends and winning lots of new customers. It was one of the smartest things we've ever done."

Brad Lawrence had the courage of his convictions. Do you?

Life is more fun on the edge.

And the view is better, too.

Roy H. Williams

4
Sensible Design

"... there is no perfect knowledge which can be entitled ours,
that is innate; none but what has been obtained from experience,
or derived in some way from our senses."
William Harvey

What does Christmas taste like? What does Christmas sound like? Smell like? Feel like? What does the experience of Christmas evoke in your senses?

Sensible design uses the concept of concurrent thinking to create ideas. We all experience the five senses at the same time; however, in many cases, people do not consciously separate the senses and attempt to feel each of them individually.

Thinking about Christmas from the perspective of each sense is simple enough, but how does sensible design translate to the business world?

Although most people have never tried to consciously think and separate the five senses in their ambiguity, senses play a huge role in consumers' satisfaction with and attraction to a product or business. Consumers evaluate products based on the way the product appeals to their senses.

Manufacturers know this. The marketing concept of branding is designed to create emotional ties between the consumer and the product. Studies show that almost 75% of our emotional behavior is derived from the sense of smell, yet a product's scent is typically ignored in favor of look and sound.[7]

Sensuality is enticing. The manufacturers of brand-name goods are just beginning to harness the power of the senses by differentiating their products through multisensoric (or Multisensory) packaging that appeals to each of the five human senses. Multisensory packaging goes beyond the traditional look and sounds of a product and integrates smell, touch, and taste into the product's casing. Research from the Milward Brown Institute has revealed that innovative packaging techniques can increase consumer's brand loyalty and generate increased sales.

In one study, consumers were asked to choose between two identical pairs of tennis shoes. The shoes were placed in two different rooms. Each of the rooms was completely identical, except that one room was infused with a pleasant scent. Consumers not only preferred the shoes in the room infused with a scent by a margin of 84%, but they also perceived the value of the shoes in that room to be almost $10 higher!

Wouldn't you think that all companies would try to identify what aspects of their product evoke a positive association with the consumer's senses and use that association to their advantage? Surprisingly enough, that's not always the case.

That's Not the Way We Do Things

Let's talk about a leading projector manufacturer who will remain unnamed here to minimize the embarrassment. Every projector in the world that I know of is advertised and sold on the basis of weight, color, luminosity, and cost. This company's projector is the best-selling projector on the market, but not because it stands out in any of the above areas. The makers of this projector have tens of thousands of customers telling them why they bought this specific product– and it's not for any of those reasons.

[7] Cyberlis blog: Brand Sense: Beware Brands Are After Your Five Senses!. http://cyberlibris. typepad.com/blog/2005/02/brand_sense_.html. Accessed 03 Mar. 2008.

Consumers choose this particular projector because it's *quiet*. This particular model happens to be the quietest projector on the market due to its unique cooling fan design.

Why is this important to business consumers? We have all been in meetings where you constantly have to move the projector away from the conference telephone because the projector is so loud; it keeps keying the microphone and the people on the other end have real difficulty hearing people talk.

This is noteworthy because the makers of the projector do not say anything about the noise level of the product in any of their marketing or advertising materials. Why?

I once asked the CEO of this company, "You've got all these consumers telling you the reason they're buying this projector is because it's so quiet. Why don't you advertise that little detail?"

He said that changing all of the marketing materials, brochures, and advertisements would be too much of a problem. Besides, he replied, "That isn't how we sell projectors. Every projector in the world is sold on the basis of weight, color, luminosity, and cost. Why change?"

I saw him about a year later at a Christmas party, and I brought the issue up again (I really do think that challenging conventional wisdom and authority is entertaining). When I got about halfway through my spiel, he said, "Didn't you already talk to me about this?"

I said, "Yeah, and your answer still sucks. Why won't you just try something new?"

I suggested that they create an advertisement on their Web site that simply says, "Our projector is the quietest projector ever built," leave the ad up for a month, and see what happens. I'm certain that the company could sell even more projectors if they used their biggest marketing tool to their advantage.

Unfortunately, they still haven't taken my advice. Every projector in the world is still sold on the basis of those same four factors – even though those product qualities aren't the only factors that convince consumers to purchase a particular model – because no one is willing to differentiate.

What Has My Computer Been Eating?

I was told this story a few years ago by an Apple Computer employee.

When Macintosh computers first came out, Steve Jobs learned a very important lesson in sensible design from a young girl. The girl was the daughter of one of Jobs's friends, and Jobs had recently given the girl a brand new Mac. Jobs asked the girl, "So what do you think of your new computer?"

The girl told Jobs that her new computer was the coolest thing in the world. She was delighted by the Mac's features and capabilities. But when Jobs asked if there was anything she didn't like about the computer, she said, "Well, there is one thing..."

"What's that?" Jobs asked.

"It stinks."

"What do you mean it stinks? You mean something about it doesn't work?"

"No, it just stinks."

"Stinks? Like what?"

"Well," she said, "it smells like a fart."

Jobs was a little confused. How could a computer smell like a fart?

When Jobs returned to Macintosh, he decided to investigate. Sure enough, he discovered that the production area did smell a lot like a fart – but why?

It turned out that when the engineers took the Macintosh computer from a prototype to production, they made an error in the timing of the curing of the plastics. The computers were built with sulfur-cured plastics, and the plastics weren't being cured all of the way. The computers were being shipped out to consumers in boxes when the plastics were only about 90% cured, hence the "fart" smell from the residual sulfur.

If Macintosh had considered their computer's design from the perspective of each sense, they may have thought about and addressed this issue sooner. Luckily for them, one little girl's keen sense of smell prevented the odor from turning off other prospective buyers.

When I apply sensible design as a brainstorming strategy, everyone in the room is asked to think about the concept from the same perspective at the same time – from the view point of our senses. We think about the concept in relation to each sense, one at a time, and generate four or five hundred new ideas.

When we start talking about how the concept feels, tastes, or smells, people usually look at me like I'm nuts. Things are usually pretty quiet at first, but by the end, almost everyone in the room starts participating and throwing ideas out there.

After we finish brainstorming, we go into our left brain and think about each idea logically. In the end, we usually find that we've generated five to ten ideas that could be easily implemented – ideas that we never would have thought of if we hadn't considered the product from the perspective of each individual sense.

Although the issues and ideas we come up with can be pretty important concepts, addressing the issue or finding a solution is often simple. The biggest obstacle to solving the problem is identifying it in the first place. Many times, no one has ever stopped to consider the product or problem from the perspective of their senses.

Find the Simple Fix

When I worked on the space shuttle program, we had an issue with the Solid Rocket Boosters during water landings. When the boosters hit the ocean after the first shuttle launch, the ocean water moved out of the way and then slammed back on the metal case and crushed it. These cases come in four pieces that cost $500,000 each. These cases were designed to be reusable, so obviously we couldn't have these expensive cases being destroyed every time the boosters landed.

We engineers, in our infinite wisdom, put these big, metal stiffener rings on the outside of the cases so they wouldn't crush. At the next launch, the water hit the stiffener ring and ripped the case up twice as bad.

Test, error, try again.

Then we came up with an idea to spray-apply an isoprene foam at a 45° angle under the stiffener ring so the water would hit the case and curve off without ripping it apart. This plan actually worked quite well, but there was one issue: the foam contained cyanide and the technicians spraying the foam needed to wear bunny suits to protect themselves from the deadly chemical.

We used the sensible design tool in our next meeting to brainstorm some ideas. Imagine sitting in a room with a bunch of engineers and NASA people and saying, "OK. Let's talk about the operation of spraying foam. How does it feel? How does it smell? How does it taste?" I get strange looks from students when we first approach this exercise in a class, but these people looked at me like I was out of my mind.

I asked the skeptics to trust me, and we began brainstorming. After we generated a few hundred ideas, we prioritized our list. The sense of feel had revealed a particularly important issue. One of the most critical things that we came back to was the idea that these guys in bunny suits were going to be unbelievably hot.

The procedure would be taking place on the sixth floor of a new facility at the Kennedy Space Center in Florida. The facility was an uninsulated, tin shed building that reached temperatures of 128° with 100% humidity in the heat of Florida's summers. The biggest problem with the plan was that the guys in bunny suits were going to pass out from the heat.

We came up with the simple solution. By installing a small venturi tube in each suits' airline, we could drop the internal temperature of the suits by approximately 50°. The modification only cost $250.

Even though the process of sensible design seems really far-fetched and freaky, we actually came up with a very practical solution to a problem that we might not have ever thought of – and prevented the guys in bunny suits from dropping dead in the heat.

The practice of sensible design illustrates an important point. Creativity doesn't have to be earth-shattering. Many times, the solution to the problem is really quite obvious once you know what you're looking for.

That Plan Just Won't Work

Just about every F16 in the world has to go to a facility at Hill Air Force Base in Utah once a year for annual maintenance and painting. Several years ago I went to the base to conduct a session about the facility and the painting procedure.

As we went through the sensible process, people were like, "What? Painting F16s doesn't taste or smell. This is stupid."

In spite of the crew's protests, we went through the five senses anyway, and soon discovered that one of the biggest challenges the crew was facing was *thirst*. The hangars are huge buildings that span hundreds of yards, and there are only a few water fountains located at the ends of the building. The crew was stuck in their stations doing their jobs. Walking to the water fountains took too long, and people were getting thirsty.

The solution seemed obvious. I said, "Put an engineering order out and have more water fountains installed."

There was an immediate uproar.

"We can't do that! Engineering orders take forever – and we don't have the funding for more water fountains."

Unfazed by their negativity, I asked, "Who's the supervisor in the room?"

When the guy raised his hand, I said, "OK, I know you have a $2,500 limit on your credit card because I know how these things work. Go buy 20 Igloo coolers, have maintenance fill them with ice water every morning, and then distribute the coolers around the facility."

My idea certainly wasn't earth-shattering, but the team probably never would have come up with a simple working solution to the problem if they hadn't used the concept of sensible design to think about their process from the perspective of each sense.

Give Your Customers What They Really Want

Sensible design allows us to think about a problem from a new perspective and generate more ideas. When we're talking about a concept, we think about how we want the product to taste, smell, look, feel, and sound. Just as importantly, we think about how we *don't* want the product to taste, smell, look, feel, and sound.

Would you want a computer that smells like farts? Probably not. Would you like to know which projector is the quietest? Probably so.

By using the tool of sensible design, we are able to extract ideas from each sense, think about the effects of each sense on the concept, and generate ideas that were previously overlooked. Thinking about a product, a concept, an idea, or an event from the perspective of the senses shakes your brain up a little bit.

Try thinking about your problem, product, business, or service from the perspective of your senses, using one sense at a time.

What if you were going to start a Cluster Balloon Ride company?

What would you want your customers to experience? What senses do you want to evoke?

Now, tackle your biggest problem with the same approach. What did you discover?

Car manufacturers understand the power of the senses. Eighty-six percent of consumers are attracted to the "new car smell."[8] What most people don't know is that the smell is manufactured. New car smell comes in an aerosol container and is sprayed into each car's cabin before it leaves the factory. When Rolls Royce learned that consumers didn't like their new scent as much as the old, they went to work recreating the "original" smell of the automobile, using the 1965 model as a prototype.

Consumers have said that sound is another important aspect of an automobile. In fact, 44% of consumers say that the sound of a car is more important than the design. The makers of the Acura TSX have actually artificially generated the "perfect closing" sound of their doors using vibrations generated by electric impulses in the door.

Packaging appeal is another important marketing area that relates directly to the senses. Jamie Leventhal is the owner of a privately held company known as Clio Designs. The company has manufactured a new line of men's shaving gel with revolutionary visual packaging.

Leventhal once stunned a Target buyer who asked how much he intended to spend on advertising by answering zero. The

---

[8] AIPMM: Product Management Articles for Product Management. Martin Lindstrom. http://www.aipmm.com/html/newsletter/archives/000164.php. Accessed 22 Feb. 2008.

buyer was shocked … until Leventhal revealed the prototype. The shave gel, known as NXT, is sold in a triangular container that glows on the shelves, inviting customers to pick up the product and examine it in greater detail. A light-emitting diode in the bottom of the container lights up every 15 seconds, stays on for a few seconds, and then fades out. The container is tinted blue, and when the batteries in the base are lighted, the product looks like a miniature lava lamp or aquarium.

Consumers are drawn to unique packaging, and retailers have expressed excitement about the new product, referring to the design as the most advanced packaging they'd ever seen. In fact, Levanthal believes the ideal location for the product is on lower-level shelves.

"When you look down at them it's more dramatic, so what I'm doing is going into retailers and saying, 'Let's take the less valuable real estate on the shelf and make it more valuable,' " he said.

By appealing to the consumer's senses, Levanthal's company has been able to eliminate advertising costs. Levanthal says that the additional manufacturing cost per unit was less than what bigger brands spend on advertising.[9]

Blue Ice Vodka is another brand that has established an image via sensory product packaging. This company uses stir sticks with a blue LED light on the end. When the stir stick is sitting in the bottom of the glass, the whole drink glows blue. I once saw this product in a martini bar, and quickly noticed that it was the only drink in the entire bar that the women were drinking.

Appealing to your customers' senses works. Do not be afraid to try an unconventional approach to your issues. Creativity

[9]Luminous packaging helps NXT product sell itself. International Herald Tribune. Andrew Adam Newman. http://www.iht.com/articles/2008/03/04/business/light.php. Accessed 04 Mar. 2008.

doesn't require genius, and your idea doesn't have to be revolutionary. Sensible design allows innovators to take their product to the next level and harness the power of the senses.

Why Most Ads Don't Work

I've said many times, "Most ads aren't written to persuade, they're written not to offend."

This goes back to chapter one, "Nine Secret Words" in my first book, *The Wizard of Ads.* Do you remember the nine secret words? "The Risk of Insult is the Price of Clarity."

Clarity. Ah, there we have it.

Rare is the ad that makes its point clearly.

The customers who cost you money are the ones you never see; the ones who don't come in because your ads never got their attention.

I was writing an ad this week and decided to insert a word flag. I chose a phrase of declarative rebuttal; "And to that, we say, 'Piffle and Pooh.'"

Obviously, "Piffle and Pooh" is just a whimsical way of saying "Poppycock."

My client was worried that people might be offended, so he asked me to change it to something else. I hung up the phone and yelled at the walls. If you're curious what I said, just walk into my office. I'm pretty sure it's still echoing in there.

Would you like to know the **4 Biggest Mistakes** made by advertisers?

Mistake 1: Demanding "Polished and Professional" Ads
If you insist that your ads "sound right," you force them to be predictable. Predictable ads do not surprise Broca's Area of the brain. They do not open the door to conscious awareness. They fail to gain the attention of your prospective customer. This is bad.

Mistake 2: Informing without Persuading
Study journalism and you'll create ads that present information without:
(A.) substantiating their claims,
"Lowest prices guaranteed!" (Or what, you apologize?)
(B.) explaining the benefit to the customer.
"We use the Synchro-static method!" (Which means…?)
"It's Truck Month at Ramsey Ford!" (Come to the party, bring my truck?)

Mistake 3: Entertaining without Persuading
Study creative writing and you'll draft ads that deliver entertainment without:

(A.) delivering a clear message.

"Yo Quiero Taco Bell" (Dogs like our food, you will, too?)

(B.) causing the customer to imagine themselves taking the desired action.

"Yo Quiero Taco Bell" (I should buy a taco for my Chihuahua?)

The best ads cause customers to see themselves taking the action you desire. These ads deliver:

INVOLVEMENT: Watch a dancing silhouette ad for the iPod and mirror neurons in your brain will cause part of you to dance, as well. This is good advertising.

CLARITY: The white earphone cords leading into the ears of the dancing silhouette make it clear that the white iPod is a personal music machine.

Mistake 4: Decorating without Persuading

Graphic artists will often create a visual style and call it "branding." This is fine if your product is fashion, a fragrance, an attitude or a lifestyle, but God help you if you sell a service or a product that's meant to perform.

"Do you like the ad?" asks the graphic artist.

"Yes, it's perfect," replies the client, "the colors create the right mood and the images feel exactly right. I think it represents us well."

Sorry, but your banker disagrees.

Hey, I've got an idea; why don't you and Artsy go home and redecorate the living room at your house? Me? I'll stay here and ruffle some feathers and sell some stuff. I hope you don't mind.

But you probably will. *Because you worry needlessly when people don't like your ads.*

Ninety-eight point nine percent of all the customers who hate your ads will still come to your store and buy from you when they need what you sell. These customers don't cost you money; they just complain to the cashier as they're handing over their cash.

Do you believe the public has to like an ad for the ad to be effective? You do?

To that I say "Piffle and Pooh."

Roy H. Williams

5
Clear as Mud

"Neurosis is the inability to tolerate ambiguity."
Sigmund Freud

Men and women both have babies.

That's a fact of life – because I just said so. If we make the assumption that both sexes are physically capable of giving birth and brainstorm for creative childcare options, do you think we would come up with some new ideas?

I actually get out a camera during my classes when we talk about this subject. If you look around the room, you'll see that the women are vigorously nodding their heads, and the men are looking at me like I'm completely nuts. But really, you haven't hurt anything by assuming that men and women both have babies. You've just gained a totally new perspective.

Now, what if I told you that the magnetic North and South Poles were going to flip? Is that illogical? Not at all; in fact, it's already happening.

On average, the magnetic poles flip every 200,000 years; however, the time between reversals is variable and it's been about 780,000 years since the last flip.[10] We can prove this by looking at ancient pottery. When the clay was spun on the spinning wheel, the iron particles in the clay acted as compass needles and pointed north. Once ancient civilizations cured the clay, they created a permanent record of where North was.[11] Ancient pottery reveals that the poles have flipped.

[10] Why Does Earth's Magnetic Field Flip?. John Roach. http://news.nationalgeographic.com/news/2004/09/0927_040927_field_flip.html. Accessed 19 Mar. 2008.
[11] Discovery Channel – Ancient China – Inventions & Technology. http://www.discoverychannel.co.uk/ancient_china/inventions/compass/index.shtml. Accessed 20 Mar. 2008.

Whether men can have babies or the North and South poles really flip doesn't matter. What's important is the fact that there's no harm in assuming they can to break up the logic and look at things differently.

The title of this chapter refers to ambiguity. One of the biggest hindrances to creativity is the fact that people do not allow ambiguity. Things must be clear-cut; right or wrong. We want specificity from life and from each other.

Engineers hate ambiguity. When I'm speaking to a group of them, someone will always stop me and say, "Okay, hold on Mark. You've got to clear things up a bit."

"No, I'm being ambiguous on purpose."

"Well, I'm not allowing my team to go through this without further clarification."

Sigh.

We avoid ambiguity because of communication problems. People want to know that they're on the same page, but in a brainstorming session, it's okay to be ambiguous. It's okay to think about other ways an idea can be interpreted.

People also get too hung up on logic. Obviously, logic is part of the creative process, but logic can be restrictive to the brainstorming session. My restrictions on logic really get under engineers' skin, too. When I tell a room of engineers that absolutely, positively no logic is allowed for one hour, their anger is palpable. I hear everything from, "you're wasting time," and "if we're being illogical how could we ever make it work," to "we don't have the budget for this kind of thing," and "this is stupid." They actually get mad.

What the engineers don't understand is that we need that one hour to be totally illogical and ambiguous. You can be logical for the other 23 hours of the day if you need to, but for one hour, withhold judgment and let the creative juices flow. (OK, I am done picking on engineers, but since I am one, I gave myself that license. This attitude is a trap we all fall into).

Judgment kills creativity. When the boss opens their mouth and says, "That won't work," the creative process dies and no more ideas get thrown out.

Ambiguity is really about interpreting things differently, letting go of logic, and escaping from the fear of judgment. To encourage ambiguity, I tell students to listen to their dreams. Dreams are some of the most ambiguous experiences we encounter in life. Do you ever wake up in the morning and think about your dreams? Are you able to apply that crazy dream to what you were working on before you went to sleep?

Of course, when I tell people to listen to their dreams I'm not encouraging them to try to steal Brad Pitt from Angelina Jolie or quit their day job to become a rock star. I want students to listen to their dreams in a more literal sense. Pay attention to what your illogical right brain is saying. If you'll remember the discussion about the lawyer and the beagle from the Introduction, you know that the little beagle is probably trying to give you an answer to what you were thinking about the day before.

If you haven't already concluded that I'm a little bit different, you're going to think so now. I'm to the point that I can connect my crazy wild dreams to what I was thinking about in my logical left brain about 50% of the time. As long as I don't roll out of bed and fully wake up, I can usually make the connection between my crazy dreams of flying around in a pink tuxedo and a problem that I've been pondering.

Comedy and Creativity

When you hear a joke that's funny, did you ever wonder why it was funny? You probably laughed because the punch line was unexpected. The climax was unusual, and did not follow a normal train of thought. Because the punch line was not what you were anticipating, the joke got your attention.

There are a lot of similarities between comedy and business creativity. Both involve things that are unexpected from the consumer's point of view.

Think about good advertising or marketing. These campaigns work best when they include an element that grabs your attention because it was not expected. Now let's look at the anatomy of a joke.

A comedian usually begins by telling a story.

> *"I got this one DUI, which was a bogus charge because it turns out they were stopping every vehicle ..."*

The comedian tells the pieces and parts of a story that travel along a predictable path. They're trying to build a pattern in your mind as they build momentum for the story. Now, based on this pattern, there's going to be an anticipated result.

What a good comedian does, especially when they're telling a funny joke, is redirect you to left field before they get to the anticipated result. The punch line will be completely different from what was expected. That's what makes the joke funny.

> *"I got this one DUI, which was a bogus charge because it turns out they were stopping every vehicle traveling down that particular sidewalk. That's profiling and profiling is wrong!"*
> *-Ron White, Blue Collar Comedy Tour*

The next time you hear a not-so-funny joke, stop and ask yourself if the punch line was pretty close to what you were anticipating. If the punch line was expected, the joke probably wasn't very funny.

Keeping the Boring and Mundane Out

Broca's area is a tiny part of your brain that serves as the gatekeeper for keeping boring experiences out of your memory. Broca's area only allows unusual, exciting, or otherwise unexpected things to be stored in your brain. If you hear a ho-hum joke, or you have a ho-hum experience with a company, you're probably not going to remember it.

In order to make a lasting impression on customers, you have to get past Broca's area. The experience needs to be both pleasurable and unexpected. If you can accomplish this, you can plant your company, its products, and its services into their memory and help trigger word-of-mouth advertising for your business.

When you're looking for a new idea or approach to your business or life, go for the unexpected.

Magic Words

Yes, there are magic words. Do you know them?

Penetrate the shield of customer indifference by shooting verbs from your word-gun. Leap the wall of inattention by putting verb-springs under your feet. Hold the gaze of a wide-eyed audience by smearing verb-honey on your lips.

Verbs are magic words. Rollicking, laughing, lollygagging verbs. Snuggling, cuddling, canoodling verbs. Prancing, strutting, swaggering verbs. Sizzle and wiggle and leap and thrust, drizzle and tickle and beep and bust, projected into the mind they must trigger a mental action.

Verbs kick open the door to Broca's area of the brain, that portal to conscious awareness. And meter doesn't hurt, either.

We're going for Broca.

Broca's area of the brain is that part of us that anticipates, and hates, the predictable. If you want to bore a person, just do what they expect you to do and say what they expect you to say. Works every time.

Broca's area is intrigued by the unexpected. And Broca is required to interpret verbs. *This is why the word most electric is an unexpected verb.*

Take the magic up a notch by Seussing.

The Simpsons – When Lisa's schoolteacher hears the town motto, "A noble spirit embiggens the smallest man," she mentions she'd never heard the word *embiggens* before moving to Springfield. Another teacher replies, "I don't know why; it's a perfectly cromulent word." Later in the episode, while talking about Homer's audition for the role of town crier, Principal Skinner states, "He's embiggened that role with his cromulent performance."

Suessing – making up your own words – gains our attention with a slap of wit. Think of it as Tabasco sauce.

Here are some Broca-surprising half-steps as you move your feet toward Suessing:

Use a noun as a verb: "Just Harley-Davidson your way to the head of the line."

Use a verb as noun: "If you can't deliver dazzle, I'll settle for twinkle."

Use a modifier as a verb: "He's planning to slippery his way through the press conference."

Use a verb as a modifier: "It's a kicking shade of pink."

Use a modifier as a noun: "I'm on the road to lethargic."

Use a noun as a modifier: "Now don't get all *Brokeback Mountain* on me."

That's enough play for one Monday Morning. We'd better get to work before our bosses doubt our cromulence and disemploy us.

Roy H. Williams

The Flat Earth Society

I once had a guy in my workshop stand up and say that my theory about the magnetic poles was absolutely, positively impossible. He said that the poles could not have flipped because the world is not 70,000 years old.

What? That same man also expressed the opinion that we've never actually put a man on the moon. Thousands of people claim membership to a group that believes that the round earth is a myth. That shocked me. I thought that there would only be like four nuts left out there, but I was wrong.

My wife is from Tennessee. When she introduced me to her father for the first time, she made the mistake of leaving me alone with him in a room. He asked me what I did for a living, and I told him that I worked on the space shuttle program.

He gave me a look and asked, "What do you *really* do?"

I thought he was looking for more specificity, so I started going into the details of my job, but he just cut me off and said, "No. Where do you really work? There is no space shuttle, so there can't be a space shuttle program."

I started laughing, but then I realized that he was serious. My father-in-law died believing that there was no space shuttle and that we'd never put a man on the moon.

Ambiguity is a powerful tool for creativity, but like all things, in the end it requires balance. In the end you can't ignore facts and data altogether either; there needs to be a balance of the two. There we go again with duality.

How Tall is That Building?

One of the major roadblocks to creative thinking is the assumption that there's only one right answer to any problem or opportunity that you're having. We all know that there are hundreds or even thousands of ideas that are better than the first idea that you came up with. Unfortunately, most people stop thinking when they come across the first idea that has any merit at all.

A better approach is to come up with a lot of ideas first. Come up with one hundred ideas before you actually pick one. Why?

Because the best way to get a great idea is to get a lot of ideas to choose from.

A student in my class once asked, "Why would I come up with a bunch of answers if I already have a solution that will work?"

I explained it to him this way. "If you were looking for a date, would you rather have three girls to choose from or three hundred?"

Then the light bulb went off in his head. The best way to get a good idea is to get a bunch of ideas first.

There is this story about a student in grade school who had to build a homemade barometer in her garage. A barometer is a tool to measure pressure. The homemade devices were just a simple design with plastic tubing filled with colored water. You can also use a barometer to determine altitude. The higher you go in altitude, the less pressure you have.

As part of the barometer project, this student had to present her barometer to the class and answer questions from the teacher. The teacher asked her how she would use this barometer to measure the height of a building. Of course, the teacher wanted her to say that she would go measure the atmospheric pressure at the bottom of the building, go measure it at the top of the building, and then use the pressure differential to determine the height of the building.

Instead, the student said, "Okay. I know how I can measure it. I would just go to the stairwell of the building and take my barometer with me. The barometer is twenty inches tall, so I can just mark off twenty-inch sections and then count them all the way to the top of the building."

"No, that's not really the answer I was looking for. How else could you use your barometer to measure the height of the building?"

"Well, I guess I could tie a string to my barometer, go to the roof of the building, lower the instrument down until it touches the ground, and then pull the string back up and see how long it is. Oh! And I know from my physics class that the equation for a falling object is □ x gravity x times squared, so I guess I could just throw the barometer off the roof, time how long it takes to smash to the ground, and then solve the equation for the height of the building."

At this point the teacher was steaming. "You're driving me crazy! You know exactly what the barometer is used for. What is the simplest and easiest way to use that instrument to measure the height of the building?" the teacher demanded in a stern voice.

Well, I don't know about you but I'd knock on the superintendent's office door and say, "Hey! Look at this cool barometer I built. I'll give it to you if you tell me how tall this place is."

Just remember, one big roadblock to creative thinking is

assuming there's only one right answer. The best way to find a great answer or idea is to generate a large selection of possibilities to choose from first.

Go for the unexpected. Don't limit yourself with logic and specificity. Ask yourself, how else can this be interpreted? By allowing yourself to be ambiguous, by allowing yourself to think about something in a new way, you'll gain an entirely new perspective – and discover a multitude of solutions to your problem.

6
View Point

"From a dog's point of view his master is an elongated and abnormally cunning dog."
Mabel L. Robinson

"Your birth mother's first name was Toni. She was 14 years old when you were born."

That was the first line of the new packet that had just arrived in the mail.

"Toni held you after birth and showed a great deal of love and concern for you. She felt adoption was the best plan as she wanted you to have the security and family life which she could not provide.

She and your birth father were boyfriend and girlfriend in high school. When you were born, he was 16.

Toni was described as a feisty, healthy kid who was very bright, but whose behavior was out of control.

The social worker speculated that had she had her parents' active support and had plans to marry your birth father, she might have raised you.

She was asked to leave the maternity home after some concerns about excessive 'necking' she and her boyfriend, your birth father, were engaged in during his weekly visits to the maternity home.

Your birth father was described as 'being on the short side of average build.'"

If you had ever met me, you would find that last statement extremely hilarious. I am 5'7 and 13/16th".

This particular package had arrived because of the sudden and unacceptable rise in my cholesterol levels last year, as mentioned earlier. This spike, which occurred in spite of the fact that I was eating better and exercising more than ever before in my life, just didn't make sense to me. Becker, my doctor, had suggested that since I was adopted and had no medical history he could refer to, I should take the safe route and get on Lipitor. But I didn't want to take any more drugs.

I also had no real desire to search for my birth parents. Now don't get me wrong. Of course I thought about my birth parents from time to time as I was growing up (or I wouldn't be curious or even human) but it was never that big of a deal to me for one very good reason: I was raised by the best and bravest parents in the world. In the 60s, they adopted four kids from four different families, God bless them. I never had any reason to search for my birth parents because I already had the greatest parents on Earth.

But then this cholesterol issue got me going. I called the adoption agency and asked if they had any medical history on my birth parents. They said they could send me a packet with "non-identifying information," if I was interested. After some thought, I said OK.

That was how I ended up with the Toni packet. Her name was Toni Gayle *something*. I didn't know her full name because they had whited out her last name on each page to make her "non-identifying."

Except on the last page. On the final page of the packet, someone had made an error and whited out the middle name, Gayle, and left her last name. McDaniel. Now I knew her full name.

Toni Gayle McDaniel.

My birth father's name was Richard Martin *something*. The last name was whited out again, but I could tell the name was five letters. Hmmm … Brown? Green?

I started to mentally peel the onion.

Then it hit me. I knew my birth father's last name was Smith.

When I was about seven, my mother (the one who adopted me) was looking for my birth certificate for some reason long forgotten. I was standing next to the filing cabinet with her as she was going through the papers. I don't think I had ever seen my birth certificate before. When she pulled the document out, I saw two names.

Mark Lee Fox … and Richard Martin Smith.

"Mom, who is Richard Martin Smith?"

She didn't know what to say at first. I think she had forgotten that there were two names on the birth certificate.

"That was the name the foster parents gave you before we adopted you."

I am certain that is what she was told or what she remembered. At the time, the name wasn't all that important, especially when you consider I was only seven.

But then, thirty-nine years later, after totally forgetting about that unimportant episode, some brain cell in the recesses of my brain remembered "Smith." Go figure.

Now what?

Knowing their names made a difference. My birth parents were now real people. That notion dramatically changed my viewpoint about my life. I started thinking differently about things I had assumed or taken for granted for 46 years, things that may or may not have been correct.

Was there a 60-year-old woman out there in need of closure? Was there a 62-year-old father in the same boat? What if I contacted her and she got angry? Would she be happy to hear from me or not? She was only 14 when I was born. What did that pregnancy do to her life? Did she even remember having a baby? I know she went to a maternity home for a while, but then what? Did her parents send her away?

What if I called her and she had a heart attack? That possibility stuck in my head for several days. "What if my phone call kills her?"

These and 10,000 other questions ran through my mind the following days and changed my view point about adoption, myself, and my life in an instant.

I use this story to illustrate an example of how a change of view point or a change of perspective can generate questions. If learning about my birth parents can raise 10,000 questions in my mind, what other perspectives can I use to generate that same burst of ideas and curiosity?

You don't have to experience something as dramatic as this to change your viewpoint. This is an extreme example of contextual change. You can change the way you are looking at an issue by looking at the idea from another person, place, or even another *thing's* view point and get a plethora of new ideas and thoughts about the issue. Using a new view point allows your creativity to flourish.

You can really get creative when you think about a topic from the perspective of something that's not human. I once read about an engineer at Sunbeam who pretends he *is* the idea. So if he's making a toaster, he imagines that he is the toaster. He asks himself, do I want people to look fat or skinny when they see their reflection in my panels? How do I clean the crumbs out of my bottom tray? By thinking about the product from the view point of the product, he is able to make a mundane task both more fun and become more innovative.

How could you change your perspective or view point in your business to generate 10,000 new questions? What if you assumed the view point of the CEO of your company? What if you assumed the view point of President Bush? What would you do differently?

Are the creative juices flowing yet?

Oh yes. You might be wondering if I ever found the medical history I was searching for. The information was listed on the last page of that fateful packet.

"Medical history: The only medical history (as follows) was provided by your foster family during the six months that you lived with them before you were adopted."

You were described as a whiney, crying, gassy baby.

Gee thanks, how helpful.

That's Total B.S.

In June 2002, Elizabeth Smart was abducted from her bedroom in Salt Lake City, Utah. She was discovered eight months later, camping with her kidnappers six miles behind her house.

While Elizabeth was missing, I wrote a proposal to the FBI committee investigating the crime and offered to come in and teach my workshop for free. After all, I'm a perfect expert. I know absolutely nothing about lost children and procedures. I thought, "Maybe I can help them think about the case from a different perspective."

I asked myself, "How would nature find her?" In the proposal, I started writing ideas of how to find her like, look for DNA in the water, enlist the Civil Air Patrol, and use satellite imaging.

Now, this may sound like Monday morning quarterbacking, but hear me out. The case took place before Google Earth was created. At that time, you could purchase any satellite image of the Earth for $149 and view any place on the planet that the Department of Defense hadn't blocked for security reasons. What if the FBI had actually done that? They might have noticed that someone was camping in the same spot for eight months. After all, in Utah no one is allowed to camp in any spot for more than 14 days.

I sent 25 e-mails and made 20 phone calls to that investigating committee, but no one ever responded. One day, I was telling this story to a class when a man stood up and said, "Mark, that story is complete B.S."

I said, "Okay ... why do you say that?"

He replied, "I know for a fact, because I was a key member of that FBI investigation."

That was a bit of a conversation stopper. What do you say to that? So I just moved on.

About thirty minutes later, the same guy raised his hand and asked if he could say something to the class.

I held my breath.

He said, "I want to apologize. I've been sitting here for the last half hour thinking about it, and I actually do remember some nutcase sending us a proposal about all kinds of crazy stuff. You're probably right about us not calling you back, but you know what?

I remember now, and we did run a *background check on you.*"

Even though the FBI clearly didn't see the merit in my plan, I still think that the view point approach could have helped them find Elizabeth more quickly. How many other ideas could they have come up to look for her? The view point of Nature alone offered several viable ideas for the search. What if they had been willing to explore other perspectives and think about how they could find a missing girl from another view point?

Seeing Yourself Real
Paper Roses Have No Fragrance

Most of us are out of balance and suffering for it. We're either too pragmatic or too romantic.

The pragmatist never stops to smell the roses. "What's the use? Just get the job done, move onward and upward. Winners never quit and quitters never win."

The romantic smells the roses and gets misty-eyed. "Roses are so meaningful. Let's sit down and talk about our feelings and listen to some music and understand."

You realize I'm not talking about actual flowers, right? I'm talking about the pitfalls of a too-flowery life and the emptiness of a life without them. I'm talking about the dangers of a lopsided perspective.

Good things come into conflict. And there is no choice so difficult as the choice between two good things.

Justice or mercy?
Honesty or loyalty?
Inspiration or accuracy?
Time or money?
Science or romance?
Which way do you lean?

A weak student will choose one side of a duality and disparage the other side while a brilliant student will stand between the poles and feel the energy that passes between them.

F. Scott Fitzgerald put it this way, "The test of a first rate intelligence is the ability to hold two opposed ideas in the mind at the same time, and still retain the ability to function."

Life is a tightrope.
Leaning is dangerous.
Balance is what you need.

"In fact, romanticism and science are good for each other. The scientist keeps the romantic honest and the romantic keeps the scientist human."
                            – Tom Robbins, *Another Roadside Attraction*, 1971

I'm not suggesting that you seek watery compromise, that mind-numbing "happy medium" cherished by the frightened and the weak.

I'm suggesting you find the electricity that flows when two poles of a duality are brought into close proximity.

Electricity is not a compromise. It is an altogether third, new thing that emerges from two potentials.

"And so I will tell them one of the greatest, perhaps the greatest story of all – the story of good and evil, of strength and weakness, of love and hate, of beauty and ugliness. I shall try to demonstrate to them how these doubles are inseparable – how neither can exist without the other and how out of their groupings creativeness is born." – John Steinbeck, *East of Eden,* 1952

Can you see the truth in opposite possibilities?
Your opponent isn't always an idiot.
Your adversary isn't always evil.
Learn to love your enemy and feel fully alive.
Reach for the electricity.

Roy H. Williams

The Universal Experience

"David, whatever you do, don't mention the 'L' word."

"What the hell is the 'L' word?"

"Shush....don't even say the letter. Don't even think about it. I'm talking about *licensing*. We don't even want to say that word. If we do, we'll have their lawyers on us like white on rice. The project will never get approved because we're too small for them to care about granting us a license. They wouldn't even give us the time of day. We'll be dead in the water. Don't you dare bring up that word. We have to figure out another approach. We need to go at this from another viewpoint."

Dave Campbell and I had been brainstorming for days on how we could leverage our new creativity and innovation course. We kept asking ourselves, how do we make this new course larger than life? Who could we partner with that could take us to a higher level of status and credibility, one that we couldn't possibly reach on our own?

We finally settled on Universal Studios. If we could partner with them and use the prestige of Universal to launch our new course, we knew we could make our class an instant success.

Our plan was to put the course together and integrate our workshop with the activities and facilities of the theme park. The class would be a three-day corporate training event on creativity and innovation at Universal Studios Orlando.

We had managed to set up a meeting with Universal to

94

showcase our product. We wanted to hold this event on Universal's property, and we desperately needed to use the Universal name in our marketing materials. Their name would give us the leverage we were looking for, but we knew they would never agree to let us license the Universal trademark.

We needed approval to use the Universal name, but we knew if we brought up the "L" word, they would just tell us to go pound sand. From Universals' view point, there was no reason to allow us to license the name. We weren't big enough. We didn't have enough revenue potential for them to care. They spill more popcorn in a day then they would make on a revenue share with us over a year.

To get approval to use their name, we knew we had to approach the issue from a different view point, so we put on our curious caps and started doing research.

We found that Universal hosted three to four corporate events at their theme park *per day*. We figured that if all these other companies were already using Universal's facilities for corporate events, we could do the same thing; we just needed to host our own corporate event.

On the day of the meeting, we were extremely cautious.

"So let me get this straight. You are the Corporate Events Organization team for Universal Studios Orlando. You already have a system set up to handle three or four corporate events each day. What do we need to do to host a corporate event here as well?

"Well, you simply select the facilities and days you want and then book your event with us. All we have to do is complete a normal purchase order."

Now I had to dance around the "L" word issue.

"OK, so the corporations that come here now ... they all have to tell their employees that the event is being held at Universal Studios Orlando ... right?"

"Yes, of course."

"So I can safely assume they post information about the event on their internal Web sites."

"I'm sure."

"They probably provide maps of the park, information about local hotels, restaurants, and general details about the event, such as what to bring, what to wear, and what there is to do in the area. They probably use some of your marketing collateral to share that information internally, as well, right?"

"Sure."

"Do you have a packet of information about Universal that we could use to announce our corporate event?

"Certainly. We can get you a package."

"And since you have more than a thousand companies hosting events here each year, do you see any problem with us posting some of your marketing materials on our Web site? You know, the Universal logos, restaurant information, and details about rides ... that sort of thing?"

"No, we don't see any problem with that."

We had just gotten approval to use the Universal Studios name without ever discussing the "L" word.

We just had to use a different perspective. Of course, we were looking out for Universal's best interest as well. Nothing we did was devious or deceitful. Not discussing the "L" word didn't hurt anyone.

We got our new event approved, and we are providing another (albeit small) revenue stream for the Universal Corporate Events team, all by using a different view point.

Check it out: www.imagination-live.com

Use View Point to Make Your Ideas Stick

Chip and Dan Heath recently released, *Made to Stick*, a book that explores why some ideas thrive while others die. I have spoken to Chip and Dan about their powerful and insightful book, particularly about how we could use a new view point to generate dozens of new products and services based on the book's principles. The foundation of the book is based on the observation that "sticky" ideas have several common attributes.

Sticky ideas are:

                  Simple
                  Unexpected
                  Concrete
                  Credible
                  Emotional
… and tell   StorieS

These attributes spell success, which makes the concepts easier to remember. Let's now explore each of these concepts in greater detail, highlighting some examples from the book.

Simple

In the military, there is a concept called commander's intent. The commander's intent is defined as, "a concise expression of the purpose of the operation and the desired end state that serves as the initial impetus for the planning process. It may also include the commander's assessment of the adversary commander's intent and an assessment of where and how much risk is acceptable during the operation."

No military plan ever survives initial contact with the enemy despite the enormous amount of planning that goes into the operation. Military operations and the environment are complex issues that are not easy to plan for – and the enemy gets a choice on what happens.

That reality makes the commander's intent even more important. This statement is a simple core message that everyone can understand: "This is the desired outcome; this is what we came here to accomplish." No matter what happens, the foot soldier on the ground knows what has to be accomplished that day.

Unexpected

As you'll recall from previous chapters, Broca's area is the portion of your brain responsible for filtering boring, mundane, and otherwise unmemorable experiences from your long-term memory. An experience, product, or event has to break a mental pattern in your brain in order to be embedded in your long term memory. The movie, "The Sixth Sense," mastered the unexpected. Throughout the film, viewers are shocked and surprised by the multiple twists. This cinematic masterpiece is memorable primarily because the creators harnessed the power of the unexpected.

Concrete

"I believe that this nation should commit itself to achieving the goal, before this decade is out, of landing a man on the moon and returning him safely to the Earth."

President John F. Kennedy, May 25, 1961

President Kennedy's challenge to Congress is memorable because there is no wiggle room in this statement. Kennedy's objective was to land a man on the moon and return him safely within the decade. The challenge was concrete and clearly defined, and thus more likely to stick in the minds of its recipients.

Credibility

Credibility has an incredible impact on the "stickiness" of a message. In *Made to Stick*, the authors discuss how the NBA brought home the dangers of AIDS to their rookies in a way that they wouldn't soon forget.

The NBA requires all rookies to meet in a mandatory session before the season begins. On the first night of the orientation, the players were hanging out at the hotel bar when a group of very attractive women walked in. The women were dressed for attention, and the players were happy to oblige. By the end of the evening, several of the players had made plans to get together with the various women later in the week.

When the players arrived for their first meeting in the morning, they were shocked to see the women from the previous evening lined up in the front of the room. One-by-one, the women stepped out of line, introduced themselves, and said, "and I'm HIV positive."

That stunt certainly added credibility to the NBA's message, but how do you think the rookies' viewpoint changed in light of the women's revelations? Their perspective changed dramatically when they realized that the beautiful women they had been flirting with the night before were, in fact, HIV positive. This new view point brought home the message that the NBA was so desperate to transmit: AIDS is real, and anyone, anywhere can be a carrier of this deadly disease.

Emotion

One of the easiest ways to make a message stick is to tap into someone's emotion. Charities have known for years that if they can make an emotional, one-to-one connection with a person, they'll give more money than they would have donated to a group fund. That's why charities often have patrons "sponsor" or "adopt" a young child in an impoverished, third-world country. By giving the donor a name, a picture, and a story of the recipient, the charity appeals directly to the donor's emotions, leading the donor to contribute more money.

Targeted messages such as these change the donor's view point as well. Even though there are a lot of people in need, when a potential donor looks at the world through the eyes of a starving child in a third-world country, their perspective changes. Charities capitalize on this new perspective by letting donors know that their money really can change one life, even if they can't save the world.

StorieS

Stories add a human element to a message, making it both more unusual and memorable. Think about Subway's Jared campaign. Almost everyone is familiar with the story of the man who lost hundreds of pounds by creating his own Subway sandwich-based diet. Jared's story has carried a lot of momentum and weight for the Subway campaign. Stories stick.

As you consider your issue from different view points, keep Chip and Dan Heath's SUCCESS attributes in mind.

The Wonderful World of Shrink Wrap

The importance of opening your mind to new perspectives and view points cannot be underestimated.

On January 16, 2003, the Space Shuttle Columbia launched into space at a seemingly uneventful launch. We later learned that the foam on the external tank, the insulation around the outside of the tank, had broken into pieces, fallen off, and struck the left side of the orbiter wing. Although nobody knew it at the time, the foam pieces had damaged the wing. Upon reentry into the atmosphere, the damage to the wing caused it to heat up and fail. Later on, we all saw the heart-wrenching videos of the vehicle tearing apart upon descent.

The Columbia's fatal reentry was obviously a horrible disaster. The loss of the crew and vehicle was a devastating blow.

Now, let's switch gears for a moment. Do you remember the Tylenol scare in the early 1980s? Seven people in the Chicago area died after ingesting capsules that had been laced with potassium cyanide poisoning. Although the perpetrator was never caught, the deaths led to reforms in the packaging of over-the-counter substances.

Do you know how many billions of dollars that the pharmaceutical industry has spent on packaging materials and processes since that case? The advances and improvements they've come up with are unbelievable. As I was examining the foam problem, I asked myself, "What outsiders could NASA bring in for a new viewpoint and perspective to help solve the problem? Why couldn't NASA bring in some packaging engineers to shrink wrap the external tank?

Shrink wrap. The idea may seem strange, but why not? We shrink wrap bales of hay, medicine, and leftovers. Shrink wrap keeps things in place. Everyone knows that you cannot open a music CD, and the child-proof bottles on aspirin make it difficult for intelligent adults to retrieve their pills.

I suggested my idea to a group of NASA officials and engineers in a lecture I presented in June 2005. After my lecture, there was a celebration for the opening of a brand-new facility. I was standing around talking and enjoying the appetizers when I decided to bring up my idea in a more personal setting.

I asked a few people, "What do you think of my shrink wrap idea?"

"Well, you know, it's not going to work because ice will probably stick to the plastic," they replied.

Well, that wasn't actually what I had in mind anyway. I was thinking about a polymer that you would spray on. My polymer would be spray-painted on to the external tank, cure at room temperature, and shrink on its own. I am sure we can find a formulation that ice won't stick to.

The conversation went on for a while, and the two men I was speaking with started looking over my shoulder and trying to figure out how they were going to get away from this nutcase. As they started to backpedal to try and escape from me, I dropped a bombshell.

"Well, you know you never used to have a foam problem back when you used to shrink wrap the tank."

That stopped them in their tracks. "What are you talking about?"

I said, "Well, you *used* to shrink wrap the external tank."

"No we didn't."

"Yes you did."

They just looked at me with a glazed expression.

"The shrink wrap was called **white paint**."

Blank looks again.

"You used to paint the tanks white. When the tanks were painted, you never had a foam problem."

"Are you serious?"

"Well, actually, I don't know if that's true or not, but you know what? **Neither do you.** There weren't enough cameras then to examine the details and see if any foam fell off or not. So the paint itself may have actually been strong enough to have solved the problem."

Even though my hypothesis may or may not have been correct, I was just trying to get them to think differently and to understand the importance of a new perspective, a new viewpoint.

Uncover Your Inner Artist

Dr. Betty Edwards' book, *Drawing on the Right Side of the Brain*, teaches people how to become better artists, while also unleashing creativity by encouraging readers to explore and familiarize themselves with the hidden potential in their own brains. So, to further explore the power of view point and perspective, I'd like to make you into an artist.

This is a five to ten-minute exercise. Go get a piece of blank white paper and a pencil. Do not turn your page upside down.

Replicate the image you see **without looking at objects**. Look at the **lines**, **angles**, **curves**, and **spaces**, paying special attention to the **relationships** between spaces, angles, and curves, and the **distance** between lines.

Remember, there are no objects. There are no eyes, there is no nose, and there is no face. You are simply trying to duplicate *exactly* what you see, not what you think you see.

Start drawing.

Seriously, put the book down and go get a piece of paper and something to draw with. Do the exercise before you read anymore. Come on! Give yourself a gift and escape to the right brain, it's only 10 minutes.

I'll wait.

When your image is complete, take your paper, turn it right-side up, and look at what you've drawn. Is your picture better than you expected?

The first time I did this exercise I was shocked. My drawing was incredible, especially when you consider that stickmen are the foundation of my art career.

The reason that your image probably looks better than the pictures you typically produce is because you changed the context. You changed your viewpoint. Rather than looking at the picture as an object, or as specific elements such as an eye, a nose, or a face, you just tried to reproduce what you actually saw, which enabled you to depict the image in greater detail and accuracy.

This idea of context applies to business and life as well. You're used to recognizing patterns and themes, but when you identify those patterns and run with them, how much detail are you missing? How much detail are you leaving out because you already have the pattern established in your mind?

Have you ever had someone finish a sentence for you? When someone does that, they are assuming based on patterns and experience that they don't even need the rest of the information in your thought because they think they already know what you are going to say. Have you ever had someone finish a sentence incorrectly or miss your point altogether because they were so stuck on their own perspective?

When you look at the image from a totally new perspective, you're not allowing your history, prejudices, or patterns to draw the picture for you.

Apply the same concept to your personal and professional life. Rather than drawing *conclusions* based on what you already know, look at the issue from a new context or view point and be amazed by what you can discover and create in your own mind.

Remember, *"From a dog's point of view his master is an elongated and abnormally cunning dog."*

Once Upon a Time

I was freshly married to Pennie and barely old enough to see over the dash of a car but I wanted to show her the magical places of my childhood, so we saved up enough money for 3 tanks of gas and made the 200-mile drive from Broken Arrow to Ardmore, Oklahoma.

I never knew my father's father. A couple of photographs and a pocket watch are all that remain of the original Roy H. Williams. But my mother's dad I knew. Roy Pylant (PIE-lant) was the iceman in Ardmore for more than half a century.

My career as an iceman began one afternoon when I was five. A restaurant called for 100 pounds of crushed ice and I went with Daddy Py to deliver it. I watched him dump the ice into the restaurant's icemaker and then I carried the empty canvas bag back to the truck. I wasn't big enough to do much else.

As I walked away I heard, "Looks like you got you a new helper."

"That's my grans-ton Little Roy. He saves me a lotta steps."

Daddy Py couldn't say "grandson" without putting a T in it.

Daddy Py's house had chickens and a little stone washhouse and a garage from which you could see the edge of the world if you climbed up onto its flat tar roof.

Once, when I was nine, Daddy Py and I took a break from crushing ice to go with Larkin from Larkin's Bait Shop. He needed to check his trot lines and asked if we wanted to go along. Trot lines were illegal, of course, but Larkin knew how to hide them so he never got caught. He got a big catfish that day and I got my first ride in a motorboat. I also saw Tucker Tower. It was even cooler than the garage at Daddy Py's house.

Summer after summer, Daddy Py and I would roll out of bed early, drive to the ice plant and slide 300-pound blocks of ice onto his '65 Chevy long-narrow pickup. *Roll the tarp over the ice, drive to Lake Murray, crush and bag the ice, toss it quick onto the truck, cover it again with the tarp and deliver it to the convenience stores.*

I was good at it.

As a child, it never occurred to me that my family spent summer vacations at Daddy Py's because we didn't have the money to go anywhere else. I figured we went there because it was the grandest place on earth. And Mama Py took care of us all.

106

Back then they didn't let you become a grandmother unless you could cook and Mama Py was a grandmother of five. Her food glowed like the sword Excalibur. Dopers would give up drugs for it. Ministers praised it from the pulpit. Shakespeare wrote sonnets about it.

Mama Py had a vegetable garden. Bright rays of color would shine from her kitchen windows as she prepared tomatoes, okra and corn on the cob with bowls of beans and fried potatoes. Her kitchen table glimmered like a leprechaun's pot of gold.

Then Daddy Py would arrive with a tinfoil bundle and 2 mysterious jars of liquid. The quart Pepsi bottle with the screw-on cap contained a thin, grey-brown au jus, redolent with coarse black pepper. The baby food jar contained an equally thin, red liquid that sparkled with what appeared to be cayenne. The tinfoil contained sliced brisket. Airplanes buzzed the house to get a sniff of it. This was Lieutenant McKerson's barbecue.

We delivered ice to him every morning.

The sidewalk in front of McKerson's was broken. The building had no air conditioner. A tightly sprung screen door traded magical aromas for outside air. There was a hole worn in the linoleum in front of the serving counter, its edges smooth, tapering down to a mirror of grey cement, the silent work of a million shoes standing, twisting, turning to leave with their tinfoil treasures and sparkling jars. I looked into that mirror and saw the soul of America.

And it was beautiful.

Rich men had tried for decades to get McKerson's recipe by offering to franchise his little place, but McKerson had no interest. He cooked for the tired, the poor, the huddled masses yearning to breathe free.

Each morning I'd hold open the screen door and Daddy Py would plunge into the mist with a 12-and-a-half-pound block of ice. I never saw McKerson's face. These early morning hours had him boiling Pepsi bottles and baby food jars in a 25-gallon aluminum pot. I saw only the white apron strings tied behind his neck and back. He didn't turn to see who we were. Our delivery of the ice was a morning ritual worn as smooth as the hole in the linoleum. We were gone in less than ten seconds. Ice is an impatient master.

One day as we drove away, I asked, "What branch of the service was Lieutenant McKerson in?"

"He was never in the military. His mama just liked the name."

A decade later I sat with Pennie, my young wife, across the street from Lieutenant McKerson's in Ardmore. Daddy Py and Mama Py were dead. I told Pennie about the Pepsi bottles, the baby food jars and the soul of America. We were gazing in silence at the tired little building when an ancient man emerged in a glowing white apron. He hung an Open sign on a hook outside. We watched as he went back in.

I sat and thought.

Then I drove away, unwilling to taint the taste of the memory.

Roy H. Williams

7
Universal Network

*"When one tugs at a single thing in nature,
he finds it attached to the rest of the world."*
John Muir

We've talked a lot about creativity, but what exactly is creativity anyway?

Creativity is bringing into being something which didn't exist before, either as a product, process, or thought. This new thing can be a combination of things that already exist – things that were not previously used or applied in the same manner. I refer to this phenomenon as combination creativity.

Combination creativity looks at the connectedness of things. Combination creativity involves looking at things that don't look like they should be combined, but somehow work together in an application that was not thought of before.

Changing the Application

Randice-Lisa Altshul was a housewife with a big idea. One day, she was tempted to throw her cell phone out the window of her car as a result of a bad connection. After realizing that cell phones were too expensive to lose or throw away, she was struck by the possibility of a disposable phone.

We've all used cell phones and phone cards, but Altschul looked at these two objects and thought, how else can these two items be used? How can I combine these two things to create something new? Altshul combined the cell phone with the phone card to create the Phone-Card-Phone, a paper phone with an integrated

109

circuit on the paper. The minutes are pre-programmed onto the circuit, and once the minutes are used up, the phone is thrown away.[12]

Altshul took two things that already existed and created an entirely new product. She wrote a proposal to Motorola asking if she could do a pilot test of her product and they funded her project. How's that for creativity?

Wendy Silver, a stay-at-home mother of two, stumbled upon another popular invention. Silver's inspiration stemmed from the frustration she experienced while trying to recreate a chopped salad that she'd eaten in a restaurant. As she painstakingly chopped each ingredient, she thought, "There has to be a better way." Silver wanted to create a tool that would allow her to chop and mix her ingredients simultaneously, without the hassle of cutting boards and knives.[13]

Silver took utensils that already existed: a spoon, a knife, and a pair of scissors, and combined them together to create the Toss and Chop. Her invention was nothing new. The Toss and Chop is merely a combination of things that already existed, yet she sold everything she had in inventory on the first day the product was sold on QVC.

The Reebok Pump, a popular line of athletic shoes in the early 1990s, is another example of combination creativity. Reebok was trying to come up with a new product line, so they went completely out of their industry for inspiration. In their search for innovation, someone explored the medical industry and found an IV bag.

The IV (short for intravenous) bag was inserted in the sole of

[12] The Disposable Cell Phone or Phone-Card Phone. Mary Bellis. http://inventors.about.com/library/weekly/aa022801a.htm. Accessed 25 Feb. 2008.
[13] Toss & Chop, salad utensils, salad chopper, salad scissors, kitchen utensils, kitchen gadgets. http://www.silvermk.com/about_us.cfm. Accessed 24 Feb. 2008.

the shoe, and they called their new creation the pump shoe. The prototype and the first shoes off the production line were actually made with real IV bags, like the ones you'd find in any hospital. The pump has since been modified, but the origins of the concept remain rooted in a product that was already in existence but used for an entirely different purpose.

The Art of Originality

Thomas Edison once said, "Originality is the art of concealing your source." Many of the greatest inventors and thinkers of our time did not create their famed inventions, but rather expanded upon what another innovator had already created.

Humphrey Davy designed the first light bulb – not Thomas Edison. Davy had the first patent on the bulb, but his design was not particularly popular because it was too bright. Davy's basic technology is actually used today in search lights.

Edison's first innovation was really the industrial research lab built in Menlo Park, New Jersey. What many people don't realize is that while many of the inventions created at Menlo Park are legally attributed to Edison, his team was actually responsible for the majority of the research and development. Edison took hundreds of people from different industries and then mixed them into a huge cross reference of disciplines and fields. His team – not him – was responsible for expanding on Davy's design to create the first indoor light bulb.

John Forbes Nash was an American mathematician who received the Nobel Prize in Economic Sciences for his work in game theory. Nash stumbled upon his prize-winning idea as a graduate student at Princeton chasing girls in a bar.

Robert Fulton, a U.S. engineer and inventor who is credited as the creator of the steamboat, also got his idea from other sources. Fulton took two things that already existed: the sailboat and the steam engine, and created the steamboat.

Albert Einstein, another widely recognized innovator and inventor, won his Nobel Prize for his theory of photoelectric effect; however, he did not come up with the idea. Max Plank, another scientist, was the first person to discover photoelectric effect.

Einstein publicly asked Plank, "Can I borrow this idea and keep developing it?" Plank allowed Einstein to develop his theory further, and Einstein was ultimately awarded the Nobel Prize for his work.

Another little known Einstein fact involves his first wife, Mileva Maric. Albert and Mileva, who was also a physicist, were separated for most of their married lives. The couple's love letters have recently been unveiled and in the letters, the couple writes back and forth about the Theory of Relativity. The letters reveal that Mileva wrote many of the equations leading up to the Theory of Relativity, but she is not credited for her contributions in any formal public record.

Einstein once said, "Many times a day I realize how much my own outer and inner life is built upon the labors of my fellow men, both living and dead, and how earnestly I must exert myself in order to give in return as much as I have received." His words take on a new meaning when one considers the contributors to Einstein's most-recognized inventions and theories.

Although Einstein, Fulton, Nash, and Edison did receive inspiration and contributions from outside sources, I am not disputing their genius. The fact remains that these brilliant individuals took something that already existed and built and expanded upon it to create something entirely new. Combination creativity *is* innovation.

I'm curious as to what percentage of Nobel Prize winners got their inspiration from somewhere else. I don't have a conclusive answer, but I estimate that up to 90% of award winners got their idea from an outside source. They admit it in their biographies. These great men and women were recognized for taking an innovation to the next level, not on the basis of how they created the idea.

After all, there is no such thing as a truly unique idea. If you think you've got one, you're kidding yourself. But that doesn't mean you can't do something fantastic with it.

Ferries and Flies

Dr. Robert Dane once sat on the docks of Australia's Sydney Harbor and thought about boats, ferries, and all the other ships in the harbor. Almost all of the ships in the busiest harbor in the world run on diesel fuel, which is a major contribution to the pollution problem.

Dr. Dane recalled reading a book about ancient insects and the evolution of how they grew wings. Common sense dictates that insects grew wings to fly. That's what I always thought. But Dr. Dane had read that insects originally grew wings to regulate their body temperature. Bugs used their wings as solar panels; they stuck out their wings to absorb the sun's radiations and used the sunlight to stabilize their internal temperatures.

Dr. Dane took the concept of a bug's wing and thought about the wing in conjunction with the pollution-free sailboat and the efficiency of solar panels. He realized that by combining these things together, he could overcome multiple obstacles. Pollution would no longer be an issue if the boats could run without diesel fuel. When combined together, the wings and solar panels would overcome the vagaries of the wind that doesn't always blow and the sun that doesn't always shine. Using solar panels and wings together would also allow the ships to get more speed than from either force alone.

You may be thinking, sure this plan sounds great on paper, but nothing realistic could ever come from that kind of pipe dream. Yet in the summer of 2000, Dane's Solar Sailor,[14] the world's first solar/wind/hybrid-electric powered cruise boat, took to the waters of Sydney's harbor. The Solar Sailor is a 20-meter-long catamaran that makes 7.5 knots without producing any water or air pollution.

What a cool idea for the environment. The mechanics of Dr. Dane's boats are not revolutionary. He just combined existing technologies with a little bit of inspiration from nature to create an entirely new concept.

Shuttlecocks and Rocket Ships

Burt Rutan is known as the aviation god responsible for creating all kinds of freaky planes. He created the Voyager, the first plane to fly around the world on a single tank of fuel, among many other revolutionary and record-breaking experimental aircraft.

In the fall of 2004, Rutan and his team won the Ansari X Prize, a $10 million award to the first civilian company that could launch the equivalent of three people into space twice within 14 days.[15]

Many people believe that the propulsion or rocket forces would be the biggest technological issue to overcome, but much of

---

[14] Olympic Champion: Sydney's Solar Sailor. Bill Moore. http://www.evworld.com/article.cfm?storyid=107. Accessed 14 Mar. 2008.

[15] SpaceShipOne captures X Prize. CNN. Michael Coren. http://www.cnn.com/2004/TECH/space/10/04/spaceshipone.attempt.cnn/index.html. Accessed 12 Mar. 2008.

that technology was borrowed from other sources. One of the biggest obstacles for Rutan's SpaceShipOne flight was reentry.

When an object is going 20,000 to 25,000 miles per hour in orbit, it will literally slam into the atmosphere upon reentry. The vehicle hits the atmosphere extremely hard and fast and slows down very quickly over a short amount of time, which creates a great deal of heat. Although there were proven reentry systems that Rutan's team could have utilized, the current systems were too heavy for his aircraft.

To solve this problem, Burt asked himself, "Rather than slamming on the brakes, what would happen if I tapped them instead? What if I reenter over a much longer period of time and make reentry a slower process to give time for the heat to bleed off?" He figured that if he could accomplish that goal, he could apply a much lighter thermal protection system that would not weigh down the craft. However, no such reentry process existed.

To solve his problem, Burt looked to the sports world. He thought about basketball, baseball, and football, but he really hit the gold mine when he considered a badminton birdie.

When you play badminton, you hit the birdie as hard as you can. The birdie flies up to the top of the net and then falls at a slow, controlled speed. The flight pattern of the birdie gave Rutan a design parameter for SpaceShipOne. The birdie enabled Rutan to not only come up with a lightweight reentry system, but also to design the craft as such that it dramatically simplifies the pilot's role upon reentry. The craft could basically navigate itself because of the aerodynamically stable design.

The SpaceShipOne technology is now licensed for use in a fleet of commercial spacecraft. The technology will be utilized by Virgin Galactic, a company that aims to be the first space tourism company to provide sub-orbital flights to the public.

The Ansari X Prize competition was designed to spur civilian spaceflight innovation, but ten million is a measly prize when you consider that NASA does not have the capabilities to complete this feat – and a NASA shuttle launch costs something like a billion each!

Think about that for a moment. One of the biggest technological accomplishments of our lifetime was solved by a fifty-cent badminton birdie.

What can you create using existing technologies and ideas? Do you think that your creativity might one day change the world?

8
Ideal Final Result

"Success isn't a result of spontaneous combustion.
You must set yourself on fire."
Arnold H. Glasglow

What happens after you come up with an innovative new idea? How do you execute your system or plan to achieve the best results?

The Ideal Final Result (IFR) describes the solution to a problem, without jargon, independent of the mechanism or constraints of the original problem. The IFR is "the ultimate idealistic solution of a problem when the desired result is achieved by itself." An IFR has all of the benefits, none of the harm, and none of the costs of the original problem.

The ideal system meets six important criteria. The IFR:

1. Occupies no space
2. Has no weight
3. Requires no labor
4. Requires no maintenance
5. Delivers benefit without harm
6. Takes care of *itself*

Ideality is equal to the sum of the benefits divided by the sum of the costs plus the sum of the harm. To increase ideality, the benefits of the concept must be increased by the solution, while the costs and harm are decreased. The goal of the IFR is an infinite positive result.

This concept can be explained by the following equation:

$$\textbf{Ideality} = \sum \textbf{Benefits} / (\sum \textbf{Costs} + \sum \textbf{Harm})$$

Ideality is a path toward perfection; an effort to continuously strive to maximize the benefits while minimizing everything bad about your product or service. The Ideal Final result would be reached if and when you have maximized the benefits and eliminated all of the bad. Essentially the Ideality equation would equal infinity.

The goal of reaching a true IFR (or Ideality = Infinity) may seem unrealistic, but the rationale for creating this desired end result is important. The IFR gets people to think out of the box for ideas. An IFR removes perceived and real barriers by forcing people to look at alternative solution concepts.

The IFR also focuses the creator's attention on *perfection* as opposed to *limitations*. By aiming for a flawless resolution from the start, breakthrough thinking is encouraged, less than ideal solutions are rejected, and discussions that will clearly establish the boundaries of the project are sparked.

How tall are you? 5'8", 6'3", 5'2"?

How often do you *mow* yourself? I mean you grew to your adult height but then you stopped. How is that possible if you don't mow yourself regularly?

It's in your DNA right? So what if you applied that same principle to the grass in your lawn? What if you planted a genetically altered grass that grew to the perfect height but then stopped? What would happen?

Instead of owning a lawnmower with the associated costs, labor, maintenance, fuel, air and noise pollution, storage, and loss of

Saturday leisure time to mow the lawn, the grass takes care of itself. You have reached the IFR; the lawnmower doesn't exist.

As you'll recall from our discussion about ambiguity, the best way to get a great idea is to give yourself a great number of ideas to choose from. The first idea is rarely your best idea, and in this case, rarely the Ideal Final Result. Searching for the IFR forces you to reject your initial, flawed plans and strive for the system that will provide the best solution.

The Ideal Final Result concept forces you to find ways to maximize the good in a problem, concept, or idea, and minimize the bad. There are several ways to look at this. One way I like to apply IFR is to assume you have *zero budget* to accomplish a task. This approach forces you to look at the available resources you have on hand and brainstorm ways to make your idea happen without spending any money.

Zero Budget

"What the hell is burning in here?" my wife demanded.

She didn't wait for my reply. She had smelled the block of wood burning in my home office all the way from hers. She left the room, returned with a fire extinguisher, placed it on the floor, and went back to her office without another word.

A recent client of mine named David McInnis (also a Wizard Academy grad) had just launched a startup company building parts via Stereolithography (SLA) and Selective Laser Sintering (SLS) – two bleeding edge technologies designed to build parts directly from 3D-CAD files by using lasers. This technology enables users to create these renditions without using any additional tools.

I submitted a proposal to the Air Force outlining a plan for

David's company to make parts for the F35 Joint Strike Fighter (JSF) using the SLS technology. The Air Force specifications presented an obstacle; they needed the parts to function at elevated temperatures of up to 270°F. This specification required that we use some new materials that Roger Spielman, the Director of Operations, and I had recently developed. We needed to test "tensile specimens" made from this new material, commonly called dog bones, at these elevated temperatures.

The problem was this: we were a startup company and we didn't own or have access to any tensile testing machines or a way to test the specimens at elevated temperatures. The testing machines are very expensive, so purchasing one of these machines was out of the question.

A company intern, Mike Sherwood, informed us that the local university, BYU, had one of the tensile testing machines on campus. We figured that his idea was worth a shot. After all, we had nothing to lose. We picked up the phone and called one of the professors at the college. We explained our situation and asked if they would be interested in letting us use the machine at a reasonable rate.

Dr. Brent Strong gave us the go-ahead to start using the machine, and even said that the school wouldn't charge us a dime right then. He added that down the road, if we needed to use the machine a lot that we could pay a very small fee.

Problem solved… or at least one of them. Now we had a machine, but still no way to test the specimen at *elevated temperatures*. The manufacturer of the testing machines does sell an environmental chamber accessory that would have allowed us to measure the effectiveness of the specimen at high temperatures, but the accessory cost thousands of dollars.

So, the next challenge was determining how to test the specimens at 270°F with no budget. What resources did we already have available to accomplish this objective?

I thought about my oven at home. The appliance reaches temperatures of up to 425°F – I know because I do all of the cooking in our family. The oven is more than twenty years old and we need a new one anyway, so I figured I could just cut the oven in half, and clamshell the oven around the tensile specimen while we tested them. That probably would have worked, but tearing my oven out of the wall sounded like a hassle. I know that your first idea is rarely your best idea, so I kept thinking, "What else might work? Is there another right answer?"

Then I thought about my photography lights. I wondered, "How hot will these lights get?" I know that they get pretty hot when I use them to shoot my videos, but I was doubtful that they could reach 270°F.

Since I am always curious, I decided to try the lights out in spite of my doubts. I'd never measured the temperature of the lights before, so I thought that maybe, just maybe, the lights would work.

I jammed a metal rod into a block of wood I'd found in my garage and stood the wood up vertically in my office. I went downstairs, got my photography lights, turned them on, and shined them directly at the piece of wood from about three inches away.

In order to track the temperature readings, I retrieved my laser thermometer from the closet. I know what you are thinking: "Ha-ha, look at that engineering nerd and his laser thermometer," but in my defense, the LT does have some real, practical uses like measuring the temperature of the air in my hot air balloon, checking the peanut oil temperature when I'm deep-frying a turkey (which as you know by now is off my diet), and other things like that.

I pointed the laser at the wood to measure the temperature and watched the readings climb: 150°F, 200°F, 250°F, 400°F ... When the wood reached 650°, the smoke started. I quickly turned the light off before I set my house on fire. I didn't want to have to use the extinguisher my wife had placed on the floor.

Wow. A simple photography light can heat a block of wood to temperatures over 600°? I would have never guessed; and I never would have known if I hadn't been curious enough to test the lights out and Try It. I'd found my solution. I simply turned the lights on my specimen, adjusted the lights' distance from the sample until the temperature stabilized at 270°F, and voila: mission accomplished.

My plan worked like a charm, and best of all, it didn't cost us a cent. What can you do with the IFR and zero budget?

Raiders of the Broken Cable

"You haven't taken me anywhere...in like...**forever**!"

"All right, M*iss Two Weeks*, we'll do something fun."

After nearly15 years of marriage, I have finally figured out one thing about my wife; if it has been more than two weeks since we did something fun together like visit a restaurant, take an impromptu road trip, or go see a movie, it might as well have been 20 years. Her "fun memory" self-destructs at precisely 14 days.

"What do you want to do?" I asked.

"Let's fly to Wendover."

Wendover is a scant little gambling town, on the way to nowhere, that straddles the Utah/Nevada border. From our home, Wendover is about a one-hour flight in my homebuilt airplane. We both like to go to Wendover periodically to play Blackjack – our game of choice because money seems to burn more like a blowtorch than a bonfire.

We were smooth sailing at 8,000 feet when suddenly the engine bellowed a blood curdling scream:

"Whreeeeeeeeeeeeeeeee!"

The RPM's shot past the red line. I immediately pulled back on the throttle to silence the screaming. Then without a second thought, I performed a textbook-perfect, calm, cool, and collected turn back to the airport with unruffled grace – a striking resemblance to the likes of Indiana Jones (this is how I remember handling it; of course, Miss Two Weeks has her own version of the story).

For the engine to over-rev like that meant I had lost the pitch in the propeller somehow. I immediately had my suspicions. Even though the design of the prop cable had worked fine for eight years, I never really liked the design.

I nursed the airplane safely back to the airport, all the while waffling back and forth on whether to declare an emergency with the FAA. I was still maintaining altitude and I figured if Indiana could get through this unscathed, so could I.

After landing safely, I investigated the cable and confirmed my suspicions. Sure enough, the clevis design connecting the prop cable to the electric servo had broken. The problem was exactly as I had figured.

I spent several weeks trying to improve the design, which was part of the original airplane kit. I had come up with several versions that were better and stronger, but each version still had some drawbacks. I just wasn't satisfied. The part was still made of plastic and I wasn't ready to soil another pair of tighty whities just yet.

Then I decided to take another view point.

I thought, "Let's start from scratch and throw away the old design. Let's look at the IFR, the Ideal Final Result. What am I really trying to do? How could I accomplish my task and maximize all the good and minimize all the bad? How can I minimize the time and cost? How could I approach the IFR equation so it got closer to infinity?"

Applying these IFR principles, I wondered how I could connect the servo to the prop with the least cost, least risk, and maximum simplicity. Then I tried to think about my surroundings and other hobbies.

This lead to several solutions, each one better than the last.

Then I hit pay dirt.

I knew from my sailing days that sailboats have all kinds of stainless steel cables that have a clevis as part of the cable assembly, and they look a lot like this design. There is no plastic in sail boat cables, either. I knew even the smallest of these cables were capable of withstanding 20,000 pounds of force; they safely hold sails in even the strongest of winds.

I measured the exact size of the servo and clevis connections, measured the length of the cable I needed, and jumped on the Internet. I found a listing for sailboat cables, did a little comparison shopping, and found the perfect cable for $30. I had already spent 20 times that in personal labor trying to fix the original flawed design.

I FedEx'd the part, installed it, and voila! I had a working cable, and more importantly, I felt confident that my next flight wouldn't require my best Indiana Jones emulation.

By searching for the IFR, you position yourself to find not only the best solution, but also save valuable time and money. Aim high, and you'll exceed even your loftiest expectations.

9
Brainstorming

"If at first the idea is not absurd, then there is no hope for it."
Albert Einstein

We've talked a lot about creativity and the "basic" tools we can use to generate new ideas and innovation. Still, many people get stuck when the time comes to be creative on demand.

Examine the illustration to the right. I'd like you to try to write three funny captions for this bubble. Go on, try it.

When I put this picture up in the da Vinci course, half of the class will start writing. The other half will put their pencils down on the paper and avoid making eye contact with me because they don't want to be called on.

How did you do? Were you able to think up three comical captions? If you're like most people, you probably drew a big fat blank – and that's not your fault.

As a society, we are not trained to come up with a creative idea on the fly. This exercise is no different than when you're sitting in a meeting and someone puts you on the spot to come up with a new idea for a marketing or business plan, or any other time when your boss throws you in a room and says, "Heads are going to roll if we don't get some creative ideas and out-of-box thinking."

Brainstorming Basics

How will you react the next time your boss throws you into an impromptu brainstorming session? Hopefully, the "Basics" that you've learned in this chapter will help you come up with creative ideas that wow your colleagues and boss, but first you have to establish the ground rules for the session so that your brilliant plan will not be ignored.

I know what you're thinking: "Rules in a brainstorming session? Doesn't that defeat the purpose?"

Most people do not set brainstorming rules before a session, but I've found that laying out the guidelines before you begin really helps start – and keep – the creative juices flowing.

This list of rules is a result of trying many, many different rules and ideas from hundreds of Web sites, authors, instructors, friends, and colleges on the subject of brainstorming. I have added a strong dose of my own experience to solidify this list. These are the ones I have found to be the most useful so far, but I am always trying new things as well. I encourage you to do the same; experiment and see what works best for you.

Brainstorming Rules

1. Generate as many ideas as possible. Go for quantity, not quality.
2. Encourage wild and exaggerated ideas, no matter how crazy, ridiculous, or far-fetched the idea might be.
3. There will be no detailed discussions about an idea, except to provide clarification.
4. Assign someone as the scribe. The scribe should write down every idea – no screening.
5. Keep a copy of the rules in plain view.
6. The brainstorming list must be visible to everyone.
7. Snowballing on other ideas is encouraged.
8. Postpone and withhold judgment of any idea.
9. Leave your titles at the door!
10. The optimum number of people is between eight and twelve, with one-third of the group being outsiders.

Rule Number One: Generate as Many Ideas as Possible. Go for Quantity, not Quality.

Remember Chapter 5? The best way to get a great idea is to get a lot of ideas to choose from. Aim to write down four or five hundred ideas in your session. The list can always be cut down and prioritized later.

Another reason I emphasize quantity over quality is because quality doesn't matter at this stage of the game. Have you ever been in a discussion where someone says something that's crazy and someone else in the room stops and says, "That won't work," or "We don't have the budget for that?" That type of judgment stops the momentum and drains brainstormers of their creativity.

Rule Number Two: Encourage Wild and Exaggerated Ideas, No Matter How Crazy, Ridiculous, or Far-fetched the Idea Might Be.

Say, "OK guys, the person who comes up with most creative idea in the next hour wins." Letting everyone know that craziness is OK for an hour, that craziness is, in fact, encouraged, will open the door to new ideas. You'd be surprised at the creativity that will flourish when you encourage crazy ideas.

Rule Number Three: There will be No Detailed Discussions about an Idea, Except to Provide Clarification.

When someone says something that's really creative, many times the other people in the room will begin objecting like crazy. Then the person who came up with the idea will try and give a twenty-minute dissertation on why the idea isn't completely nuts. Because the idea doesn't fit the normal patterns of business conversation, the person feels responsible for defending the merit of their suggestion. Do not allow this to happen. Each person is allowed 10 to 15 seconds to explain the concept if it is really bizarre and unfamiliar to the rest of the group, but they are not allowed to carry out a detailed conversation until the session is over.

Rule Number Four: Assign Someone as the Scribe. The Scribe Should Write Down Every Idea – *No Screening*.

I have to emphasize the second part of this rule because screening happens all the time. Everyone's shouting out ideas and somebody will say something really crazy, and the scribe won't record their idea because they believe it's too far-fetched. Make certain that the scribe understands this rule.

Rule Number Five: Keep a Copy of the Rules in Plain View.

The rules should be readily visible to everyone in the room. If anyone tries to overstep the boundaries and shoot down a rule, point to the list and politely tell the naysayer to shut up.

Rule Number Six: The Brainstorming List Must Be Visible to Everyone.

Don't let the scribe hide their list away out of sight. Everyone should be able to see the ideas that have already been generated. The list might provide the inspiration necessary for the next great idea, which brings me to my next point.

Rule Number Seven: Snowballing on Other Ideas is Encouraged.

As you learned in the Universal Network chapter, there are no original ideas. Many of the greatest innovations of today are the result of someone piggy-backing on another person's ideas. Even if an idea is only 10% different than another idea, say the new thought out loud and write it down. That 10% difference might be enough to make someone else think about the idea differently and allow them to expand upon the concept even further.

Rule Number Eight: Postpone and Withhold Judgment of Any Idea.

Judgment is one of the biggest creative killers that exists. Judgment is even worse when it comes from a higher-up. Almost everyone has been in a situation where someone throws out a crazy idea and the most senior person in the room makes a face, raises an eyebrow, or makes a deprecating comment. Suddenly, there's dead silence. I was once in a meeting when the Chairman of the Board stormed into the room and angrily demanded, "What ******* SOB came up with this ridiculous, stupid idea?" How many people would you guess raised their hand? What do you think that did to the team's creativity?

Rule Number Nine: Leave Your Titles at the Door.

This is the hardest rule for bosses. Whenever you do a brainstorming session, there is no vice president. There are no directors, bosses, or owners. I teach a lot of sessions in the military, and when I get to this rule I have to look at the highest ranking officer and say, "Are we clear? Do you understand that you are not the boss for the next hour? I want you to be fully, totally, consciously aware that you are the person who is most likely to kill the creativity in this room."

I almost have to embarrass the most senior person in this room so that I can make it clear that they're probably going to mess the session up. To bring home this rule further, I sometimes set a camera up in the room from a distance and really zoom in on the manager's face without telling them. The camera records their facial expressions and body language in response to really creative ideas. I play the video back for them over lunch on the big screen and point out their expressions. I ask them, "Don't you think your attitude hinders the creative process?"

Rule Number Ten: The Optimum Number of People is Between 8 And 12, with One-Third of the Group Being Outsiders.

This one is the biggy, and unfortunately, the least practiced in business. The critical part of this rule is bringing in outsiders. Get people from outside your department, your company, or better yet, people from an entirely different industry to sit in on your session. Companies rarely ask outsiders to join them, but outsiders offer a unique View Point that insiders cannot see. Consider this: every company in the world has problems with cost, employee retention, and other common business issues. Your problems are not unique; everyone has very similar issues to deal with. An outsider might be able to shed some light on your company's particular obstacle.

Most people think this rule won't work because outsiders will not be interested in sitting in on a session, but the reality is that everyone wants to exchange ideas. Well, the smart ones anyways. Try implementing a "brainstorm exchange" program with another company. Both companies will benefit from the experience.

Setting rules for your brainstorming session will enable you to come up with more creative ideas and solutions for your business.

Back to Basics

The "Basics" that we've discussed in Part I: Peel the Onion, Try It, Sensible Design, Clear as Mud, View Point, Universal Network, and Ideal Final Result, are the foundation for establishing a creative mind-set. I believe that Lenny, Hank, Buck, and Walt all used these basic principles as well as hundreds of other creative geniuses. However, I am fairly certain all of them would have had different names for the basics if they tried to describe how they thought and behaved. Most of them probably never tried to describe what they do in concrete concepts because they just thought that way subconsciously. With these basics, we can all do it consciously.

These basics cannot only be used in business, but in your personal life as well. The next time you're buying a car, a home, planning a vacation, or trying to figure out how to manage your teenage daughter, try thinking about the issue from the perspective of these basics.

Using these tools can make a world of difference in your ability to think up creative ideas and solutions. I've been through a number of creative thinking courses. I've had a great time dancing and singing, putting paper cups on my head, and swimming through swamps at these workshops, but when the fun is over and I come back and sit down at my desk, I often discover that I didn't learn anything that I can apply in a real-world setting.

I strive to give my readers and students deliberate methods and deliberate tools to generate ideas quickly so that they can come up with some crazy, wonderful, new ideas of their own.

In Part II we will examine the 40 Answers, which will give you a set of even more tangible, tactical tools for generating new creative ideas.

But first, a little more play.

Paid to Play

"I'm going to fix the space shuttle myself."

That is the most arrogant statement you'll ever hear me make, especially when you consider that I am no longer on the space shuttle program and I haven't been for the last ten years.

The foam issue on the Columbia mission has always been on my mind. Despite the doubts of the NASA officials I talked about in the View Point chapter, I still believe that a sprayable polymer shrink wrap would keep the foam intact and prevent debris from causing another tragic disaster.

I wrote a one-page proposal outlining my idea and sent the document to several senior NASA managers. One of them said, "Well, I was on both the Challenger and the Columbia investigating committees. I'm sure we thought about this, but I don't remember the details or what happened to that plan."

Having worked on the program, I suspected that an idea like this might have gotten lost in the lower levels of the review process and been killed before it could be thoroughly evaluated.

Not one to give up easily, I sent my proposal to another top NASA official. She suggested that I turn in a proposal for SBIR Funding – Small Business Innovation Research. SBIR funding is designed to encourage collaboration between the public and private sectors and stimulate technological innovation opportunities for small business owners. So I submitted my proposal and had a couple of months to wait before they awarded contracts. During this time, I wanted to find a cheap way to start testing my idea. I wanted to "Try It" and get ahead of the game.

In order to test the feasibility of my shrink wrap plan, I needed samples of the foam used on the Columbia shuttle. I called a friend of mine at Kennedy Space Center and asked for the specification for the foam. He gave me the NASA spec number, which wasn't very much help. I needed to know who actually manufactured the foam, because NASA wasn't just going to send some to me if I didn't have a contract. My friend went back, did some more research, and then he called and said the foam was manufactured by Pratt & Whitney.

I know that was unlikely, since Pratt & Whitney doesn't make chemicals like that, at least that I know of. After several days of research, I discovered that Dow Chemical made the foam. I visited their Web site, started doing some research, and discovered that the foam used on the space shuttle Columbia is the same stuff sold in a can at Ace Hardware by the name of Great Stuff. I called Dow and spoke to an engineer who confirmed this. Great Stuff is a sealant for doors, windows, and cracks, and can be bought for less than $10 a can.

Who would have guessed? I could now start testing several shrink wrap materials with the foam before the contract even started, just to get a jump on things.

Get Your Own Free Money

The next time you have an idea, a concept, or a business plan that you think just might work, look and see what type of funding you are eligible for. Any small business can do exactly what I did with the SBIR program, and that small business can be a company of one: you. In fact, the largest percentage, 40%, of SBIR awards go to companies with less than 9 employees. The United States Small Business Administration (SBA) Office of Technology runs the SBIR and the Small Business Technology Transfer (STTR) Programs. These programs are designed to ensure that small, innovative businesses are able to contribute to the federal government's research and development efforts.

The goal of the program is to translate scientific discoveries into products and services that touch people's lives. Vaccinations, nano-engineering techniques, laser technologies, night vision goggle simulators, robotic surgery assistants, software for spacecraft operation and control, and a new long-life battery are all innovations that began in the SBIR/STTR programs.

Your chances of getting a grant are pretty good; one out of seven get funded from every agency. Many federal agencies with large budgets have to fund the SBIR program, so if you have an innovative new plan for getting things done, check out the SBA programs and see what type of funding you might be eligible for.

Agencies that participate in the SBIR/STTR programs include:

- Department of Commerce
- Department of Defense
- Department of Education
- Department of Energy
- Department of Homeland and Security
- Department of Transportation
- Environmental Protection Agency
- National Aeronautics & Space Administration (NASA)
- National Science Foundation
- U.S. Small Business Administration
- Department of Health and Human Services

Visit www.sbir.gov for more information on the SBIR/STTR programs, or visit www.grants.gov to find and apply for other federal government grants.

On the next page, you'll find my initial one-page proposal that got things rolling.

EXTERNAL TANK SHRINK WRAP

Provide a shrink wrap type material for the Space Shuttle External Tank to eliminate all foam debris

TARGET: To utilize the extensive experience of the packaging and polymer industries to provide a material and process to shrink wrap the ET foam and eliminate debris

- Improve the safety of all future Space Shuttle missions
- Minimum impact to current operations
- Provides a fresh independent assessment and solution to the problem
- Supports NASA's Small Business Strategic Initiatives

In 1982 the Cook County Medical Examiner's office found several cases where Tylenol had been intentionally contaminated with cyanide. This was the spark that infused billions of dollars into the packaging industry and its technology. Aspirin bottles, Music CDs, soft drinks, and millions of products now have state of the art tamper-proof designs. These same materials and processes have been used to wrap and protect almost every product imaginable. The technology advancements in this field have increased many orders of magnitude in the last 20 years.

This phase 1 study will investigate this industry to determine if a readily available material and process exists that would allow the Space Shuttle External Tank (ET) to be shrink wrapped in a strong, durable, and lightweight protective "cocoon" to eliminate the possibility of any foam shedding during launch, thus eliminating the potential of future orbiter damage. The Ideal Final Result (IFR) would be to provide an off-the-shelf, lightweight, sprayable polymer that would room temperature cure and shrink, yet would not require any changes to the current foam insulation material specifications, processes, or inspections. This material would be applied as a final step in the ET manufacturing process just prior to shipment of the KSC. "Visualize an automobile painting process." This would have minimal impact to the current STS operations and would greatly increase mission safety.

Mark L. Fox is the CEO of SAAF, LLC., is a Chemical Engineer, and MBA, and will be the principal investigator of this study. Mr. Fox was part of the Space Shuttle Program for over 15 years and was a Chief Program Manager as well as a Chief Engineer at Thiokol and is intimately familiar with the program and NASA policies and procedures. Mr. Fox is currently a successful entrepreneur in several industries.

FINANCIAL: This phase one study is estimated at $70,000 for a 6-month time period.

STATUS: SAAF, LLC. stands ready to conduct this study immediately. A more detailed proposal and test plan will be submitted upon NASA's request.

ACTION: NASA to review this proposal and contact Mark L. Fox, SAAF, LLC. regarding their level of interest via a phone call. Mark will travel to NASA to meet and discuss this further at the agency's request.

Mark L. Fox, July 5th, 2006

CEO, SAAF, LLC.

Part 2 – The Tactics

10
The Lenses of TRIZ

"Everything should be kept as simple as possible, but not simpler."
Albert Einstein

Genrikh Altshuller, or Hank, as I like to call him, was a Russian engineer, scientist, journalist, and writer who once embarked on a mission to establish a set of generic rules to explain the conception of new, patentable ideas. After studying hundreds of thousands of patents, Altshuller discovered that there are only about 1,500 basic problems, each of which can be solved by applying one or more of the 40 Universal Answers.

Altshuller called his theory TRIZ, the Russian acronym for the Theory of Inventive Problem Solving. He referred to the solutions as principles, rather than answers. His original intention for TRIZ was to solve engineering and design issues; however, the principles of TRIZ are now being successfully applied to both social issues and business dilemmas. TRIZ is a set of tools, or as I like to call them, *lenses*, for generating innovative ideas and solutions.

I refer to the 40 Answers or Principles as lenses because most people find it easier to examine the problem when they can look through the magnifying lens of TRIZ to see the solution. I encourage people to ask themselves, "Which lens can I use to solve this problem?" or "How would I solve this problem if I were looking at it through this lens?"

In contrast to brainstorming techniques that rely on random idea generation, TRIZ is designed to create an algorithmic approach to the invention of new systems and the refinement of old systems.

At the foundation of TRIZ is this underlying principle:

"Somebody someplace has already solved this problem (or one very similar to it). Creativity is now finding that solution and adapting it to this particular problem."

TRIZ relies on three basic findings:

1. Problems and solutions are repeated across industries and sciences. The classification of the contradictions in each problem predicts the creative solutions to that problem.
2. Patterns of technical evolution are repeated across industries and sciences.
3. Creative innovations use scientific effects outside the field where they were developed.

A thorough understanding of TRIZ involves learning the repeating patterns of problem solutions, the patterns of technical evolution, and the methods of scientific effects, and then applying the TRIZ patterns to a specific solution. The chart below illustrates this process in simpler terms.

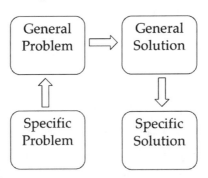

A fundamental element of TRIZ lies in the recognition that contradictions should be eliminated. These contradictions are broken into two categories:

1. Technical contradictions, or classical "trade-offs" are an obstacle to the desired solution because something

else in the system prevents the desired solution. In other words, when one thing gets better, another element gets worse. For example:

    a. The product gets stronger (good), but the weight increases (bad).

    b. Service is customized to each customer (good), but the service delivery system becomes more complex (bad).

2. Physical or "inherent" contradictions are situations in which one object or system has contradictory, or opposite requirements. For example:

    a. Software should be complex in order to include many features, but should be simple enough for the average user to learn.

    b. Coffee should be served hot, but cold enough to prevent burning the customer.

Altshuller said, "Inventing is the removal of a technical contradiction with the help of certain principles." He believed that in order to develop a "method" for the process of inventing, the individual must examine a great number of inventions, identify the underlying contradictions, and formulate the principle used by the inventor to remove the underlying contradictions.

The problem with TRIZ is that the concepts are usually taught by PhDs who get too caught up in the technical definitions. The principles are complex, and most educators do nothing to simplify them for the average person in need of real answers.

However, Ellen Domb is a friend and colleague of mine, and even though she is a PhD (we will try not to hold that against her), she is one of the few people who really understands the depths of TRIZ and how to communicate them. For those readers who want to dig really deep into the principles, I suggest visiting Ellen's Web sites; www.triz-journal.com and www.trizpqrgroup.com. She has certainly helped me.

Create your own Answers

When I teach TRIZ, I want the opposite of technical definitions. I want liberal definitions, and I encourage people to use whatever definition works best for them. I give my students license to use very liberal definitions of the lenses, so they can maximize the creativity of their answers.

TRIZ can be used in applications beyond problem solving. The lenses of TRIZ demonstrate how to approach relationships and societal problems, as well as how to be creative in your view of the world and its underlying problems.

In the pages that follow, you'll find the technical explanations of each principle, *my* definitions of the 40 Answers, and real-life applications of each lens. In some cases I have left the original definitions from Altshuller to demonstrate how some of the original, technically-focused principles are too hard to swallow, but don't worry; I break them down with a broad range of examples to make the concept much easier to understand.

Also at the end of each lens I have included some very brief additional examples called "TRIZ Bitz" to help you imagine just how many different ways the lenses can be applied.

Once you understand the definitions and see the broad range of examples you can then focus these lenses on your issues. TRIZ gives you a tangible and tactical set of tools for your creativity.

11
Segmentation

Segmentation involves breaking an object into independent parts or fragmenting things; basically, segmentation is a transition to the micro-level.

Segmentation can be accomplished several ways, for example:

1. Dividing an object into independent parts.
    a. i.e. Breaking down the writing process of a novel into chapter milestones

2. Making an object easy to disassemble.
    a. i.e. Sectional furniture that separates into parts

3. Increasing the degree of fragmentation or segmentation.
    a. i.e. Replacing solid shades with mini-blinds

Denim Fads, Firefighting, and Corporate Subsidiaries

What do denim fads, firefighting techniques, and corporate subsidiaries have in common? All are examples of segmentation applications.

Stonewashed Jeans

Stonewashed jeans are an example of segmentation as a solution. The stone-wash finish is achieved by filling an industrial-sized clothes washer with large, segmented rocks and new denim jeans.

During the wash cycle, the cloth fibers are pounded and beaten by the rock fragments, resulting in a worn-out appearance. The process also increases the flexibility and softness of otherwise stiff fabrics such as denim.

Fight Fire with Mist

Most people do not realize that fire is not the biggest cause of destruction to a burning building in many cases. The water used by firefighters to extinguish the flames actually causes the most damage. When firefighters pump thousands of gallons of water into a building, the water does more harm than the fire itself.

Mist is a more effective fire extinguisher, and causes much less damage than water sprayed from a high-pressure fire hose. Segmenting the stream of liquid into a mist of small water particles increases the good and decreases the bad, bringing firefighters closer to the Ideal Final Result. Many automatic fire suppression systems operate on this principle.

Corporate Subsidiaries

A corporate subsidiary is essentially the segmentation of a big conglomerate into smaller profit centers. A conglomerate is a company that has partial or full ownership stakes in a number of other companies, firms that may be in the same or different industries. By dividing the conglomerate into smaller profit centers, the business becomes easier to manage and control.

Animals and Autism

Temple Grandin's book, *Animals in Translation: Using the Mysteries of Autism to Decode Animal Behavior,* explores the idea that autistic individuals can better relate to and understand the way animals think and feel because of similarities in their brain development. She argues that individuals with autism cannot see the big picture. Rather, these individuals see things as segments – pieces and parts of an entire object. Grandin believes that animals think in the same way. Grandin herself is autistic, so she has a unique "view point."

Grandin's theory is that the part of the brain that is underdeveloped in an autistic person is naturally much smaller in an animal's brain. In fact, she believes that autistic people think more like an animal than another human being in terms of brain development. She describes the natural brain segmentation that occurs in autistic people and explains how this segmented thought process has worked to her advantage.

Grandin's work has revolutionized the reform of quality of life and humane killing of the cows, pigs, and chickens that humans consume. Her checklists for the humane treatment of animals are utilized by meat processing plants across the country. Fast-food chains such as McDonald's, Kentucky Fried Chicken, Wendy's, and Burger King purchase their meat exclusively from plants that have been certified by Grandin.

In relation to business innovation, her book raises several important questions. How can you think like an autistic person or an animal to solve the problem? By looking past the big picture into the pieces and parts, can you find a better solution?

I've utilized segmentation in my training courses to great success. My video newsletters are an excellent example of a segmentation application. Before I began creating the videos, I struggled to find an effective means to transmit the information to the masses. Big training videos were hard to sell because they were too long and difficult to watch and absorb in one sitting.

My Sly as a Fox video newsletters are now 3 to 5 minute, bite-sized segments. In the videos, I make my point, offer a few relevant examples, and stop. Segmenting the course into consumable tidbits was a great solution. My clients enjoy the short video clips much more than 1-hour training DVDs.

TRIZ Bitz

1. Your typical SWOT analysis in business: Strengths, Weaknesses, Opportunities, Threats
2. Different product or service offering for each target market
3. Let members of a broken family go their own ways

How can you look through the lens of segmentation to solve an issue in your business or personal life?

The Glass Ceiling

Every business that tries to rise to its full height will bump its head on a glass ceiling they didn't realize was there.

That glass ceiling is created by the business owner's core beliefs about the customer.

Traditionally, 5 out of 10 customers will be in transactional shopping mode. The other 5 will be in relational shopping mode.

Shoppers in transactional mode are looking for information, facts, details, prices. Their thoughts revolve around the product itself, not the purchase experience.

Relational-mode shoppers are looking for a pleasant experience. They want to find the right place, the right person from whom to buy, an expert they can trust. *Meanwhile, the transactional shopper is gathering the information that will allow them to be their own expert.*

A customer can be a relational shopper in one category and a transactional shopper in another. The labels don't define the customer. They describe only the mode of shopping, the momentary mind-set of the decision maker, the type of ad to which he or she will respond.

Here's what's currently happening in America:

One of the 5 relational shoppers has begun to think *transactionally.*

The reasons are:
(1.) concerns about the economy,
(2.) access to information via search engines.

Americans spent $29.7 billion online at Christmas (Nov. 1 to Dec 31,) approximately $100 for every man, woman and child in the nation, up 19% from the previous year. In other words, there was *$100 fewer dollars per person spent in brick-and-mortar stores in your town* than was being spent just a few years ago at Christmastime.

And for the first time in the history of Starbucks, traffic is in decline.

Starbucks has always sold relationally. We pay for the atmosphere of the café with its half-lit earthtones and iconic logo - the *idea* of affordable luxury - as much as we pay for the coffee. But some of us have begun to compare the quality and price of the coffee itself to the quality and price available from other providers.

Beginning to get the picture?

148

Starbucks has found the glass ceiling. In other words, they're selling as much coffee as can be sold relationally.

I'm sure you have your own idea about how Starbucks should respond to their decline in traffic, but the point of today's memo is this: A glass ceiling exists when you overestimate the number of people who prefer to buy *the way you prefer to sell.*

People never really change their mind. They merely make new decisions based on new information. Will Starbucks give us new information, a new perspective in 2008, or will they just whine at their marketing department for the inexplicable decline in traffic?

More importantly, what new information will you deliver in 2008? (You realize this memo isn't really about Starbucks, right? I don't care about Starbucks. I care about you.)

The Tiny Giant is that 1 relational shopper in 5 who is moving to a transactional perspective. This effectively shifts the marketing balance from 5/5 to 6/4. This doesn't sound like a big thing until you realize that 6 is 50% more than 4.

Do you have the clear answers that 6 in 10 shoppers demand? Are you willing to provide the growing tribe of transactional shoppers with the information, facts, details and prices they expect?

Or will you simply demand that your marketing team deliver more customers in relational shopping mode? (Please, I'm begging you for your own sake, don't fall into the trap of believing the answer is to "target" relational shoppers through some magical mailing list, e-mail list, or sponsorship package.)

Think about it, won't you?

Your financial future hangs in the balance.

Roy H. Williams

12
Taking Out

The second lens of TRIZ, Taking Out, involves separating an interfering part or property from an object, or singling out the only necessary part or property of an object. In other words, you remove the problematic aspect of the system or object, leaving only the necessary phases or pieces of the product.

When you examine your issue, product, system, or problem through the Taking Out lens, you should ask yourself, "Is there something I can take out of this product to increase the good and minimize the bad? Is there a way that I can remove all extraneous parts or phases and keep only necessary components?"

Fiber Optics, Franchises, and Free CDs

Examples of the successful application of Taking Out are abundant. For instance, have you ever sat in an office that overlooks the building's generator? If so, you'll know that the generator is a noisy disturbance that interferes with your daily routine. When you examine the generator problem through the Taking Out lens, you ask yourself, "What can I take out or take away to solve the problem?"

Take out the interfering pieces and leave only necessary components. You don't want the generator; you just want the power. Why not move the generator 100 yards away from the building and run the electrical cable underground?

Follow the Light

Fiber optics is another example of the Taking Out principle. An optical fiber is a glass or plastic fiber that guides light along the length of the cable or cord. Fiber optic technology has taken out all of the machinery and mechanisms that generate the light, leaving only the light itself. The light, the necessary component, is kept in the core of the fiber and the machinery, the interference, is removed.

The removal of external mechanisms allows fiber optic technology to be utilized in a variety of applications like endoscopic surgical procedures, Christmas tree lights, and to illuminate department store showcases using only one light source. If the machinery were left intact and not removed from the fiber optic cables, the technology would not be as versatile and many of the current applications would no longer work.

Franchise Me

Franchises are another example of this lens. In a franchise the marketing, startup costs, and training requirements are removed from the business plan. Many of the traditional aspects of owning a business are "taken out," because the franchise owner has created a complete mini-business.

The result is a simplified business model for franchisees, one that incorporates only necessary parts.

Cash Wrap

I've used the Taking Out lens to simplify the purchase process of my CDs during my creative courses and workshops. Many speakers, presenters, and performers sell their work at a table in the back of the room. Ask any of these people what the biggest obstacle to making the sale is and I'll bet they'll point to the cash wrap process. In other words, the collection of money in a product transaction is a pain.

Have you ever stood in a long line at the end of a show or workshop, waiting patiently for your turn to pay? After a long session, all you really want to do is go home and relax, so waiting 10 or 15 minutes to swipe your credit card is not fun.

Many people don't want to deal with the hassle and stand in line so they just leave empty-handed instead. I noticed this issue at many events and wondered how I could solve the problem.

I asked myself, "What can I take out of this process to simplify things?" I finally concluded that the best solution was to remove the cash wrap process entirely. During my lectures, I tell the audience that if they want to buy a CD they can just pick one up on their way out of the room and leave. On the back of the CD, I list a Web address they can visit to pay for their purchase.

Although my plan was shocking to many people, I've actually found that taking out the payment transaction was quite effective. I looked at the cost ratio of the CDs and determined what percentage of people actually have to pay for the product to break even. Ninety-five percent of the people who take a CD visit the site and pay me. They take the CD home, hand it to their secretary, and say, "Pay this guy."

No hassle, no lines, same profit. Problem solved.

Frameline Magnetism

Frameline magnetism is a tool that has been used by artists and photographers for centuries to help pull their audience into the picture. Frameline magnetism engages your mind in the composition. This is achieved by not including, or taking out, the details. Roy Williams uses famed photographer Robert Frank's work to illustrate this concept.

If you look at Frank's photographs, he captures the moment – but he leaves out the details. The result is that you are drawn into the picture because you can't tell what's actually going on or what is taking place at the event. The phrase, "tip of the iceberg," describes this concept very nicely because like an iceberg, the details of the photo are under water. You only see a portion of what's really going on.

Let's take this concept and apply it to marketing and advertising. R&R Partners is the marketing agency responsible for creating the incredibly successful Las Vegas advertising campaign, "What happens here, stays here." The playful television campaign the firm developed depicts ambiguous vignettes that suggest some sort of illicit activity, but leaves it to the viewer to decide what really happened.

Let's look at another example of this concept, one that practically everyone in America is familiar with. The Got Milk? campaign, created by Goodby, Silverstein & Partners in association with the California Milk Processor Board, was another hugely successful advertising campaign. The firm created the powerful advertising images without going into excruciating detail or specifications about milk or making a list of a hundred points of why milk is good for you. They just said, "Got Milk?"and allowed people to rely on their own interpretation of why milk is good for you. Consumers fill in the benefits of milk on their own; they don't need the benefits explained in explicit detail.

In both frameline magnetism and the Taking Out lens, you're frugal on the details. Unnecessary information or details are taken out – leaving only the necessary components.

TRIZ Bitz
1. Take the mystery out of copyright law (big opportunity for some lawyer out there)
2. "Green-Home Consultants" to help you take out energy waste in your home
3. Taking out carbon dioxide emissions from coal burning plants by pumping the flue gas through carbon dioxide-eating algae

What can you "take out" of your product, process, or service to simplify the system?

Ready. Angle. Frame.

Advertising begins only after you win the attention of your target, a difficult thing to do in this overcommunicated world.

May I suggest you do it like the Great Ones?

When you're ready to tell your story, **choose an angle** of approach.

Then **frame the scene**. Decide what to include, what to **leave out**:

Specifically, leave out:
1. anything the listener already knows or can easily figure out for themselves.
2. the name of the business anywhere it would not appear in normal conversation.
3. unsubstantiated claims.
4. clichés.
5. complicated ideas.
6. comparisons.
7. self-congratulatory pronouncements, such as "We're the number one..."
8. statements that reflect your awareness of a competitor.
9. any promise you might fall short of delivering.
10. adjectives that are not essential to the clarity of the message.
The strongest ads use simple nouns and verbs with a minimum of modifiers.

Choosing an angle is a bit trickier. You must find a perspective to introduce a new reality. Don't just add incremental knowledge to what's already known. Introduce a thought that will stand taller than any other figure on the horizon of the mind. It's like setting the stage for a Broadway production, and it can always be done in a single sentence.

Here's a glimpse of how it's done by the Great Ones:

"It came down to this: if I had not been arrested by the Turkish police, I would have been arrested by the Greek police."
> – Eric Ambler, the opening line of *The Light of Day*

"My first act on entering this world was to kill my mother."
> – William Boyd, the opening line of *The New Confession*

"There was a boy called Eustace Clarence Scrubb, and he almost deserved it."
> – C. S. Lewis, opening line from *The Voyage of the Dawn Treader*

"He was one hundred and seventy days dying and not yet dead."
– Alfred Bester, the opening line of *The Stars My Destination*

"You are standing in the snow, five and one-half miles above sea level, gazing at a horizon hundreds of miles away."
– Roy H. Williams, the opening line of *a radio ad written for Rolex*

Did you notice how I slipped myself into that list of the Great Ones? I wouldn't usually have done it but this is Monday and on Mondays I'm ebullient. It's only on Tuesdays that I'm modest.

Most people like me better on Tuesdays.

Here are some typical opening lines from average ads. Compare them to the lines that come from unusual angles and better frame the new perspective:

Typical: McMorris Ford is having a Clearance Event!
Unusual: *We want to get rid of this new truck even more than you want to own it.*

Typical: Harvey Chevrolet is Going Out of Business!
Unusual: *Here at Harvey Chevrolet we're tired of being average, so here's what we've decided to do.*

Typical: Save up to 70 percent at Neederman Optical!
Unusual: *New eyeglasses cost like stink. You know it. We know it, too.*

Typical: Leroy's Lawn Service has served the people of this city since 1972.
Unusual: *Life is too short and wonderful to spend it cutting your own grass.*

Typical: Juanita's Mexican Café at the corner of Fifth and Madison serves authentic Mexican Food from 8AM till 8PM daily.
Unusual: *So you think you've had Mexican food, heh, Gringo?*

Choose an unusual angle of view and leave out the obvious. These are the keys to opening the mind's eye. Do it when writing ads. Do it when making presentations. As with every other archetypal truth, the principles will remain unchanged. Details of their application will be the only difference.

Ready. Angle. Frame. Harness these ideas and your thoughts will gain speed and momentum.

Pow.

Roy H. Williams

13
Local Quality

"Newsworthy does not necessarily go to the worthy," proclaimed Dean Rotbart.

We had just started Day One of the incredibly intriguing Academy course, "Newsroom Confidential," taught by Dean, a Pulitzer Prize-nominated journalist for the Wall Street Journal, and I was already awestruck by how inaccurate conventional wisdom is in regards to the world of Public Relations.

Rotbart's session was truly an eye-opening experience. Throughout the two-day course, Dean's ideas continued to scream "Local Quality," although I'm pretty sure he had never heard of TRIZ. Like most of the great minds, Dean was applying these principles unconsciously.

Below is just one of his insights into the PR world:

Know Me or No Me
By Dean Rotbart

I borrowed the headline for this column, 'Know Me or No Me,' from the March 2002 edition of Continental Airlines' in-flight magazine.

The catchy title caught my attention on a recent speaking trip to New York, where the subject of my remarks, as it often is, was how companies and executives can get more positive news stories written and broadcast about them.

Based on all the money and staff resources

that large publicly held companies devote to media relations, you'd think they'd be awash in positive press. Most aren't.

Indeed, getting good press is seldom directly correlated to the size of the wallet you are willing to empty on public relations firms, PR newswires, fancy schmancy press kits or even high-paid media consultants such as me. When it comes right down to it, Know Me or No Me, is really the complete answer to successful media relations.

Companies and PR agencies seldom take the time to really get to know the news organizations and journalists who they are pitching. Communications executives are so busy doing PR the wrong way, they can't make the time to do it right.

But media relations is a misnomer.

Good press, in reality, is built on one-to-one relationships. What the rest of the "media" think doesn't count.

When you have a story you'd like to place with a national news organization, you only have to make two correct decisions to succeed.

1) Which news organization is most likely to WANT this story? (Not which news organizations do I most want to cover my story?)

2) Which reporter at the correct news organization is most likely to WANT this story? (Not which reporter would I most like to have cover this story?)

That is it! Everything you need to know to succeed at media relations. Know Me or No Me. The rest, as they say, is commentary.

As I mentioned previously, Dean's wisdom relates directly to Local Quality.

Local Quality involves changing an object, system, or service so that the product has different features in different environments. As Dean explained, the best press releases are tailored to the publication and the journalist. The writer understands their audience's likes and dislikes, and in the case of the press release, the initial audience is the reporter or editor. Although the press release is written with the ultimate goal of distribution to the masses, the release must first make its way past the gatekeeper. To accomplish this, the Local Quality of the release must appeal to the gatekeeper.

The lens of Local Quality is usually applied in one of three ways:

1. Change an object's structure from uniform to non-uniform, or change an external environment or influence from uniform to non-uniform.
   a. i.e. Using a temperature gradient rather than a constant temperature

2. Make each part of an object function in conditions most suitable for its operation.
   a. i.e. Creating a lunch container with special compartments for hot and cold or solid and liquid foods.

3. Make each part of an object fulfill a different and useful function.
   a. i.e. a Swiss Army Knife

Catering to the Audience

Local Quality plays a role in every industry, not just public relations. Almost every object, process, and system can be modified so that it has different functions in different environments or appeals to a specific, unique audience.

Look at a standard #2 or mechanical pencil. When people are writing or sketching on a piece of paper, they usually need two tools: a writing utensil and an erasing device. With that in mind, most pencils have two components, each intended to fulfill the user's specific needs. The tools used to complete each function are centrally located, with the lead at the bottom and the eraser at the top.

Adjustable wrenches are another application of Local Quality. The tool can be modified to fit whatever bolt size you are currently working with. Rather than forcing consumers to purchase many different-sized wrenches for different-sized bolts, someone came up with the idea to enhance the Local Quality of the tool to make it suitable for multiple uses.

Precision fertilizing also applies this principle. Farmers analyze their soil and put down a different fertilizer recipe based on that specific area of soil's needs. Each area of the farmer's land receives the exact combination of nutrients and fertilizer necessary to produce the greatest crop output.

Surfing the World Wide Web

I use the lens of Local Quality in my Web site design and content. I have several versions of the site, each one customized for visitors of a specific foreign country. The local quality of the site has to be modified to make sure that the content and appearance of the site will appeal to the cultural needs and preferences of users. That way, the site will be just as attractive and informational to a visitor from Chile as it is to a visitor from Brazil.

I spend a lot of time (probably too much time) tweaking the site and changing the colors, content, and design to make the page's local quality effective regardless of the culture and language of the user.

Local quality allows you to tailor and customize your product, process, system, or service to meet the specific needs of your customer. The product has different features in different environments, so that you are able to provide the functions or features your clientele need most.

TRIZ Bitz

1. Add a joke to your presentation that specifically resonates with that particular audience
2. Offer basketball tickets for a local team's game as an employee reward
3. Use of Google Maps to find a local hot tub supplier

How can you use Local Quality to improve your product and anticipate your customer's needs?

Do You Lean Toward
Niche Marketing?

Think too deeply about customer profiling and you'll soon fall into niche marketing.
And the problem with niches is they're not created equal.

Have you chosen a niche too small?

Reis and Trout inadvertently popularized niches in their extraordinary 1981 book, *Positioning: the Battle for Your Mind.* That book taught us to consider the strengths of our competitors and the "positions" they occupy in the customer's mind before embarking on our own journeys of self-identification. But many who read *Positioning* saw it only as a treatise on niche marketing. They were wrong.

Chris Anderson openly celebrated niches in last year's book, *The Long Tail,* which was likewise misunderstood. Tragically, the seductive logic of niche marketing makes perfect sense even when it does not apply.

Here's a classic example:

A dentist in a small town came to me for consultation. He no longer wanted to see 6 or 7 patients a day who required only a thousand dollars worth of dentistry apiece. He had chosen a niche and wanted me to create a marketing strategy whereby he would see only 1 or 2 patients a day who required 10 thousand to 30 thousand dollars worth of dentistry each. "And make sure that all of them have the money. Lots of people need that much dental work, but most of them don't have the money."

I fear he left disappointed. There just aren't enough rich people with bad teeth in the average small town. My friend had chosen a niche too small.

Some of my clients serve larger populations that allow us to successfully target a niche. But when onlookers see this success and assume the same strategy will work in their own small towns, the niche-devil shows his horns.

Considering a niche? Do the math.
Be detached and objective. This isn't a time for wishful thinking.

If your marketplace isn't big enough for niche marketing, you can still embrace (1.) **positioning**, and (2.) **persona-based ad writing**, a technique that speaks to personality type and appeals to a significant percentage of readers even when those readers are randomly chosen.

Persona-based writing is built upon *a customer's preferred style of buying.*

Niche marketing is built upon *your own preferred style of selling.*

Positioning is built around *the strengths of your competitors.*

Each of these is a decision-making technique, a perspective we bring to the creative process.

Persona-based writing is about *your customer's personality,* not their demographic profile. To what personality types are your ads currently written?

Positioning is about *the realities of the marketplace.* Your competitors occupy positions in the mind of your customer. Do you recognize these positions, or are you navigating with your eyes closed?

Niche marketing is about specialization, focused inventories, narrow training, *becoming the king of an available kingdom.* But before you plop your heinie on the throne, be sure the kingdom you've selected has enough subjects to provide you the living you desire.

Advertising cannot create population.

Please don't let anyone tell you that it can.

Roy H. Williams

14
Asymmetry

The lens of Asymmetry is usually applied in one of two ways:

1. Change the shape of an object from symmetrical to asymmetrical.
   a. e.g. Installing a flat spot on a cylindrical shaft to attach a knob securely

2. If an object is asymmetrical, increase the degree of asymmetry.
   a. e.g. Change circular O-rings to oval cross section to specialized shapes to improve sealing

This principle can be used to make your product, process, system, or service more attractive to customers, more unique, or to improve functionality in design.

Differentiation and Functionality

There was once a wedding cake designer in one of my courses who examined her product through the lens of asymmetry. She began to question why all wedding cakes were symmetrical, and decided to change the shape of her cakes. Her asymmetrical wedding cakes were certainly unique, but they also served a larger purpose: to differentiate her business from the competition.

Now consider musical instruments. While many instruments are symmetrical in design, those instruments that vary in shape are more distinguishable and noticeable from their standard counterparts. Remember KISS' guitars? The shape of their instruments was half the show. Something as simple as changing the shape of their guitars made the band a much more memorable act.

Shape can also be modified to improve the usability or functionality of an object. Hinge pins have been used on ships for hundreds of years. The pin needs to be tight when inserted, but should also be easily removed. Unfortunately, the pin design accomplished the tight fit, but removal was a chore. It took a very long time for someone to realize that putting a taper on the pin would solve the problem. By changing the shape of the pin, the functionality was improved.

Asymmetry does not apply exclusively to objects. For instance, a business's budget can be asymmetrical. Different departments get different financial plans and monetary awards. Rather than distributing a uniform budget plan, corporations can distribute the funds unevenly or asymmetrically to best suit each department's needs.

An Incorrect Example

"When you stock the Baja 7-packs of beer, lay them on the side with the tops of the bottles facing toward the customer. Right now you have them standing vertically and the customers can't really see the difference between the Baja brand and a normal 6-pack. I want to try this for one month and see how big a difference it makes in sales. I really think that turning the cases on their side will make the brand stand out more."

"OK, I can see how that would probably make a difference. I never really looked at it that way," said the Albertson's grocery store manager. "By the way, how long are you in town? I didn't see an e-mail or anything saying that corporate marketing was even going to be here this week."

"Oh…well I am not from corporate marketing."

"Sorry, I just assumed...which department are you from?"

"I don't work for you guys, I am just a customer."

Laughter and surprise rolled into one.

I told him that I teach creativity and innovation for businesses and that I am always curious about things and how to make them better. I said "Come on, just try my idea and see if the new display impacts sales. I am certain it will."

I have showed this example to a few other PhDs that teach TRIZ and they all tell me that this example is a horrible example of "Asymmetry" because the 7-pack is still symmetric; the case is in the shape of a hexagon. Well, of course they are technically right, but who cares?

As you learned from my brief stint as a corporate marketing adviser, the lenses do not have to be applied literally to be successful. To me, asymmetrical just means do something different with the shape. That's *my* definition. You have the license to use the most liberal definition of these 40 lenses as you like. I believe that the more creative the definition, the more creative the solutions you'll come up with.

By the way, sales of Baja increased by 50% that month.

TRIZ Bitz
1. An asymmetric trumpet mouthpiece that enhances musical range
2. Adding a single passenger side car to a motorcycle
3. Warfare in which the combatants have markedly different military capabilities and the weaker side uses non-standard tactics such as terrorism

Modifying the shape or symmetry of your product can differentiate your product from the competition and improve functionality. If you look at your business or problem through the lens of asymmetry, what do you see? Can you change the shape to make things work better?

15
Merging

"Everybody called him Pepto, because every day at work he'd have a pint of vodka in his back left pocket and a bottle of Pepto Bismol in the right. Throughout the day he'd retrieve the bottles from his pockets, take a swill of vodka, and then chase the liquor with a shot of Pepto."

"Are you serious? He was drinking while he was working?"

"Oh yeah. This was back in high school and we were just a bunch of rednecks working on the factory floor."

I had asked my friend Dave to tell me the story about the time when he used to *auction off his paycheck* on payday.

"Well, every year at church we would auction off a car. One of the guys in the church owned a local Ford dealership and he would donate a car to the church auction. Every year people always thought they would be the lucky one to drive the car home."

"I ran the auction for the church, so I was very familiar with the auction process, where to get the ticket rolls, and stuff like that. I'm also from Louisville, a huge betting community where we were always betting on the horses (Dave always pronounces it as "haarses"). One of the guys in accounting was even a bookie."

"On the factory floor I drove a forklift. There was a ton of stuff to move around the floor, so I was constantly moving from station to station delivering parts. Well you know my personality and how chatty I am; I knew everyone in the building so I would always stop and talk to the other workers as I was making my rounds. I was in a position to talk with people all day long."

"Then one day, without a lot of thought, I just decided to auction off my paycheck. I mean I knew a lot about auctions, I was used to betting, and I had access to everybody in the company on a daily basis. It was a no-brainer."

"So I drove around on the forklift every Tuesday morning yelling, 'Hey everybody, I am raffling off my paycheck, come get your tickets!'"

"How much was your paycheck in those days?"

"About $125 a week."

"How much did you sell the raffle tickets for and how much did you take in?"

"The tickets were a buck each and minimum ... I mean minimum, I would take in $250, although I usually made more like $350-$400....all tax free! On payday, I would take the lucky winner to lunch at the GE Bar and Grill. The place was a total hole in the wall. Anyway, everybody went there to cash their checks on payday. I'd buy the winner's lunch, cash my check, and then count the winnings out loud to the lucky winner *in front of the entire lunch crowd* ... twenty, forty, sixty, and so on."

"That's hilarious!"

"Here's the kicker. The previous week's winner was the first person I'd hit up for the new raffle. The winner would always buy a minimum of $5 worth of tickets, lots of time $10. Then

I would hit up all the other previous winners, and finally I'd make my rounds to the rest of the folks."

"So basically, you looked around at all of your available resources and merged them together. I mean you had auction experience, knew about betting, and talked to people all day long. You took your available resources and merged them together to come up with something new."

"Yeah Mark, I would say that is spot on."

"You know Dave, you probably didn't realize this then, but you were using some of the TRIZ basics and the Merging lens. Remember in my workshop when I explained that you should look at all the available resources you *already have* around you?"

"Well now that you mention it, yeah I do."

Like we have discussed throughout this book, a lot of the great thinkers probably have never heard of TRIZ (for most the concept didn't exist yet) or ever realize they were applying the principles. Because we are not all capable of understanding these principles unconsciously, the intention of this book is to give you a set of tools to help you *consciously* apply creativity and innovation principles the way the great ones have been doing it *unconsciously* throughout history.

By the way, Dave went on to be a senior executive at GE, among other great things.

The technical definition of the Merging principle involves either:

1. Bringing or merging identical or similar objects closer together, or assembling identical or similar parts to perform parallel operations.
    a. i.e. Personal computers in a network

2. Making operations contiguously parallel; bring them together in time.
    a. i.e. A mulching lawnmower.

Circuit boards are an excellent example of the Merging lens. In a circuit board, you're merging multiple functions into one location rather than leaving each control in its own place.

The Internet is also ripe with examples of merging. "Mashups" are the merging of two existing applications to make something new. For instance, somebody took one application, a directory of sex offenders, and overlaid the directory with Google Maps. Users can punch in their zip code and see a visual map of all the sex offenders in a particular location.

Fast-food chains have also taken advantage of the benefits of merging. KFC, Taco Bell, and Pizza Hut can often be found partnered in pairs under one roof. The advantage of the merger is that each restaurant can use the same staff, soda fountain, cooking equipment, and location. Two different brands use the same resources and cater to customers from one location.

As you can see, merging brings things closer together to improve the product or system. The applications of merging go beyond tangible objects, though.

Cashing in on the View

Let's talk for a moment about the Sydney Bay Bridge. Clearly, this landmark is beautiful, but I want to talk about one entrepreneur who wanted to *sell* the experience of climbing the bridge. People don't actually climb the bridge; they walk up the rainbow-type arches to the very top of the bridge. The person who came up with this idea is a man named Paul Cay.

This story is not only about marketing, merging, and packaging your product; it is also a lesson in using persistence to get what you want. Perhaps the most important thing to take away from this story is this:

**If you have a truly unique and
creative idea and people don't hate it,**
they weren't listening.

Folks who have been to my workshops or lectures have undoubtedly heard me say this. I'm told that Paul presented his idea for a bridge climb business to Sydney's city governments and various other bureaucracies. The board came back with a list of 60 reasons why he couldn't do this business. Most people would give up if somebody threw 60 roadblocks in front of their idea, but Paul was persistent. He needed a couple of years to make his comeback, but he eventually returned to the naysayers and said, "Is it still the same 60 reasons why I can't do this business? Because I have a solution for all 60 of them now."

He presented his rebuttals to them and after a review process they decided there was no good reason he couldn't start his business. So in October 1998, the business was officially launched: bridgeclimb.com.

There was an initial $2 million investment in the bridge for safety cables, harnesses, communication equipment, and that kind of thing. Two million may sound like a lot, but I'll let you calculate the return on investment.

People pay $160 each to do the climb. In eight years, more than 2 million people have climbed to the top. You do the math.

The original idea seemed so unbelievably simple, yet Paul's idea has won more than 33 awards to date. The business actually won its first award for the "Best New Tourist Attraction" before the climb program even opened.

The bridge already existed, and with a modest investment they turned the bridge into one of Australia's biggest tourist attractions. I've thought about this company a lot. What is their product? What are they really selling?

They're selling a *view*. And this view is not in the form of oceanfront property that can only be sold to one person. This is a view that you sell to new customers again and again every day. It's a cash cow.

TRIZ Bitz

1. Splice a lemon and lime tree together to make a "limon" hybrid fruit tree
2. One rich family introduces their daughter to another rich family's son
3. Use of traffic lights on merge lanes for major highways to improve flow

Think about your own existing products and services. Is there a way to package them differently to have a greater effect? Maybe there's a popular or famous landmark that you can partner with to get more exposure. Who can you merge with to create your own cash cow?

16
Multifunctionality

Multifunctionality makes a part or object perform multiple functions, thus eliminating the need for other parts. For instance, imagine a toothbrush with a handle that contains toothpaste or a child's car seat that converts into a stroller.

When you look through the lens of multifunctionality you should ask yourself, "What can I bundle with my current products or services to increase their value?"

One-Stop Shopping and Multi-Purpose Shoes

Multifunctionality is everywhere. If you visit a Wal-Mart or Costco store, you'll find a gazillion different products and services. You can do your grocery shopping while your car gets serviced, take your kids in for an eye exam, get a haircut, develop pictures, and fill your prescription. These stores bundle products and services into a one-stop shop and service center.

Beer packaging has also become more multifunctional. Many beer boxes now also serve as coolers. You go to the store, pick up a 12-pack, fill the box with ice, and voila! You have a collapsible cooler to keep your beer cold.

Another great example is the combination printer, copier, fax, and scanner machines. Rather than purchasing four different pieces of equipment, businesses and individuals can purchase one machine that is capable of performing all four functions.

In Florida, flip-flops have a rather unique secondary function. Every 20-year-old kid in the state has a pair of flip flops that double as a built in bottle opener. The manufacturers molded a little piece of aluminum tab and molded the tab into the bottom of the shoes. This company has dominated the flip-flop market by adding one simple function to their product. This tab probably added about $1/100^{th}$ of a cent to the cost of the product.

Even people can be multifunctional. I own a company of one – me. I am the marketing guy, the creative guru, the administrative assistant, CEO, customer service specialist, and financial planner for my firm. I am a multifunctional machine.

TRIZ Bitz

1. Stanley Multifunctional pen that combines a black ballpoint pen, a non-drying orange highlighter, a lead pencil, a stylus for PDAs, and a ruler with inches and centimeters on the side
2. A scarf that can be worn in a number of different configurations to provide a high level of comfort, protection, and style during outdoor and recreational activities
3. A cosmetic powder that enhances skin color, softens skin, and removes oil

What can you do to make your product or service fulfill multiple functions? Can you add value to your product by making it multifunctional?

17
Nested Doll

The Nested Doll principle is usually applied in one of two ways:

1. Place one object inside another; place each object, in turn, inside the other.
    a.   i.e. Measuring cups or spoons

2. Make one part pass through a cavity in the other.
    a.   i.e. An extending radio antenna

Bill Gates and the Nutty Guys

Perhaps the most obvious application of the Nested Doll lens is Microsoft Windows. Windows has built a monopoly-like empire on this principle. Windows, as the name implies, is simply windows inside windows inside windows. There are multiple screens you can see inside of one computer. Each window is "nested" within another window.

Retractable presentation pointers are also an example of a Nested Doll application. The pointer is actually several pointers, one within the other. The design allows the pointer to extend and retract so that the user can point to a graph or PowerPoint slide on the wall while standing a few feet away.

Another company, Nutty Guys, a Salt Lake City-based nut distribution firm, greatly expanded their business inside of an independent grocery store. The company carries 275 varieties of nuts, seeds, candied nuts, trail mix, and dried fruit products. The founders, two college buddies, built a creative display rack to market their product – and essentially created a store inside of a store.

Similarly, there are several applications nested within the Internet that are examples of a unique product nested within an existing product or system. Netflix is an independent company that operates and relies entirely on the Internet. Skype is also nested within the Net. Skype uses Voice Over IP (VOIP) technology that allows users to make telephone calls using only their Internet connection. With unlimited calls for $30 *a year*, they generate a hell of a lot of word of mouth.

TRIZ Bitz

1. Topkapia in Istanbul has a fig tree growing inside an evergreen as a marketing attraction
2. Place undercover forces inside of terrorist cells
3. The "Beer Belly" is a neoprene fake belly you place inside your shirt to sneak your choice of beverage into movies, concerts, and ball games (yes, it's real – www. thebeerbelly.com)

When you look at your business or product through the Nested Doll lens, ask yourself, "How can I place one object inside another to improve efficiency or make my product more user friendly?" You might be surprised by the creative ideas you'll uncover.

Ronald, Bill and You

I thought Bill Clinton was a good president for the same reason I thought Ronald Reagan was good; both were excellent head cheerleaders.

Their politics, personalities and characters were different, but each had a similar ability to keep things from spinning out of control.

Every organization has a head cheerleader.
Their business card usually says "manager."

The head cheerleader's job is to keep talented hotheads, sycophantic suck-ups, whining excuse-makers, moon-eyed lunatics and plodding paranoids all headed in the same general direction. They have to make everyone feel like everything is going to be all right.

Are there really people who can do this job?

Thrown into the deep water at 26, I was possibly the worst manager ever to assume the position. But over the years I've had a chance to observe the great ones, and I've noticed an unusual but recurrent characteristic: *Great managers are rarely excellent at any of the things they manage.*

Great coaches are great, not because they were superstars, but because they know how to awaken the star that sleeps in each of the players around them.

Great managers don't show you photos from their own vacation, they ask to see the photos from yours. And it makes them happy to see you had a wonderful time.

Great managers look for things to praise in their people, knowing that it takes 7 positive strokes to recover from each negative reprimand. Think about it. If in seven out of eight encounters we receive an authentic, affirming comment, a bit of happy news or a piece of valuable insight from our boss, we love to see them coming down the hall. But if the typical encounter leaves us deflated, discouraged or scared, our hearts sink when we see the manager coming.

Do your people love to see you coming? If not, begin looking for things to praise. Keep your ratio of positive comments 7 times higher than your negative ones and they'll soon begin to smile when they see you appear. Their newfound attitude and confidence will bring new levels of productivity. And all because you believed they could do it and made them believe it, too.

Great managers are never afraid to hire people better than themselves.

Each of the 217 times David Ogilvy opened a new office for Ogilvy & Mather, he left a set of Russian nesting dolls on the desk of the incoming manager. When the manager removed the top half from the largest of these bowling pin-shaped dolls, he or she found a slightly smaller doll inside. This continued until the manager came to the tiniest doll and retrieved from its interior what looked to be the note from a fortune cookie: *"If each of us hires people smaller than ourselves, we shall become a company of midgets. But if each of us hires people bigger than ourselves, we shall become a company of giants. –* David Ogilvy."

Now walk down the hall and find a sleeping superstar disguised as a plodding paranoid. For each of the next 21 days, compliment that person every time you see them take a right action.

Then prepare to meet a whole new employee on the 22nd day. Don't be surprised if they have the same name as the plodding paranoid that used to stink up the place.

Go. The hallway awaits you.

Roy H. Williams

18
Weight Compensation

The principle of Weight Compensation, or Anti-Weight, is used to solve a problem or improve a product in one of two ways:

1. To compensate for the weight of an object, merge it with other objects that provide lift.
   a. i.e. Use helium balloons to support advertising signs

2. To compensate for the weight of an object, make it interact with the environment using aerodynamic, hydrodynamic, buoyancy, and other forces.
   a. i.e. Hydrofoils lift the ship out of the water to reduce drag.

In other words, this principle allows you to adjust your product or system to compensate for an existing weight. As you'll recall from Chapter 10, an important aspect of TRIZ is the idea that contradictions have to be eliminated.

Weight compensation solves a classic technical contradiction or tradeoff. For example, a product may get stronger, but the new components increase the weight. Using the lens of weight compensation, the inventor or entrepreneur can find a solution that counteracts the added weight, thus solving the technical contradiction.

Sink or Swim

Submarines use the principle of weight compensation to float both above and below water. Subs float because the weight of the displaced water is equal to the weight of the ship. The displaced water creates an upward force known as a buoyant force. Buoyant forces act opposite to gravity, thus keeping gravity from pulling the craft down.

Ballast or trim tanks, which can be filled with either water or air, allow a submarine to control its buoyancy and sink or surface on command. When the submarine is floating on the surface of the water, the tanks are filled with air; thus the sub's overall density is less than that of the surrounding water. When the sub goes under, the air is released and the tanks fill with water. The water in the tanks causes the sub's overall density to exceed that of the surrounding water, allowing the sub to sink.

Companies use the lens of weight compensation all the time to move inventory. Slow moving inventory can be bundled with a hot product. Because people want the hot product in the first place, the slow merchandise add-on adds perceived value. People feel like they're getting more, and will often pay a higher price for the bundled product even though they probably wouldn't have purchased the slow merchandise alone. This trick works wonders for getting rid of inventory sitting in a back room taking up space.

The Best Bonus Feature Ever

A friend of mine, Phil Baker, has a great story that exemplifies the weight compensation principle.

Phil was 17 and had a 1965 Dodge Dart convertible he wanted to sell. He said the car was a nice vehicle at one time, and ran just fine, but by the time he wanted to sell it there was hardly any paint left on the body and the car looked terrible.

He put the car up for sale and waited a few weeks, but he didn't have any takers.

Phil also had a younger sister. All of his buddies were constantly begging Phil to set them up on a date with his sister, but he wasn't having any of that.

Then one day he put two and two together. What if he bundled a date with his sister with the car?

He spread the word around about his new and improved "product," and told his friends that if they would buy the car, he'd get them a date with his little sister. The next thing he knew, he had three or four different eager buyers. Two of the guys actually came up with the cash for the car.

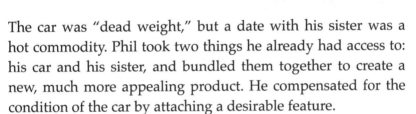

The car was "dead weight," but a date with his sister was a hot commodity. Phil took two things he already had access to: his car and his sister, and bundled them together to create a new, much more appealing product. He compensated for the condition of the car by attaching a desirable feature.

Salary v. Profit Sharing

Much like the other lenses, the principle of weight compensation is not restricted to tangible objects or literal interpretation. For example, consider the difference between a salary and profit sharing. Both provide financial benefits to employees, but the two different forms of compensation each carry a weight.

Sometimes a fledgling business owner will want my help, but can't afford my salary. When this situation arises, I often give the business the option to forgo the salary altogether and instead give me a percentage of their profits. A combination of salary and profit sharing can also be utilized.

TRIZ Bitz

1. Carbon credit trading system for greenhouse gas emissions
2. Computer time-memory tradeoff where the memory use can be reduced at the cost of slower program execution, or vice versa
3. Al Gore lifted his popularity by attaching himself to global warming

How can you make your product or service better by compensating for the weight, whether literal or figurative, of another object?

10 Unusual Ways to Advertise

Are you a one-person company with a lunch-money ad budget?

Good News: Time and money are interchangeable. You can always save one by spending more of the other.

When money is tight, spend time.
(If you don't have any money AND you don't have any time, then you're spending your time on the wrong things.)

The key to low-budget advertising is to focus on small groups and individuals.

Here are some ways to do it:

1. Door-hangers on Doorknobs. If your target is geographically defined, print doorknob-hangers and hang them on doors in your area. Results will be proportionate to the strength of your offer. So make your offer detailed and specific. "Join us for worship this Sunday morning" is less likely to bring visitors to a church than "Single Parent Support Group meets Wednesday nights at 7:00. Childcare provided." When I was young and in the seamless guttering business, I'd walk yard-to-yard diagramming rooflines on estimate sheets. The homeowner came home to find taped to their door a schematic of their roofline with my detailed bid for what it would cost to install seamless guttering on their home. Worked like magic. COST: Ink, estimate sheets, and shoe leather.

2. Flyers under Windshield Wipers. If you need to reach the drivers of a specific type of vehicle, such as pickup trucks, what better way than to walk your doorknob-hanging shoes across parking lots putting flyers under windshield wipers? Yes, you'll occasionally get run out of a parking lot by a security guard in a golf cart and some lonely soul who needs a life will call to complain that you're ruining the environment, but the results are usually worth the hassle.

3. Purchased Word-of-Mouth. Ride up and down in the elevators of tall buildings, stand at bus stops, wait at crosswalks or hang around in coffee shops to tell strangers about your business. "Have you heard about _____? It's awesome." It sounds nuts, I know, but it works. Pay a kid or do it yourself.

4. Virtual Showroom. Convert your website to a virtual showroom. Use it as an instantly deliverable, interactive brochure when people call to ask details about your company, your products or your services. "Are you sitting in front of a computer? Good. Now go to BlahBlah.com. Yeah, that's me. Now click the button that says 'Equipment.' See that second photo?" Think of this website as a place where you sit down to talk with interested prospects. Make sure the virtual showroom is equipped with all the same tools and props as your physical showroom. You'll be shocked what it does for the conversion rate of inquiries.

5. Nighttime Silhouettes. You've probably never seen one of these... which means no one else in your town has seen one either. First, locate a tall wall in a part of town that has lots of traffic at night, especially foot traffic. Then arrange with the owner of that building – and the building across the street – to let you install a logo projector. They're effective and cheap. In some situations you can even use an old slide projector to achieve the desired effect.

6. T-shirts and Vests. My little ad firm with its 41 offices worldwide was launched in 1978 with a T-shirt advertising a thought-for-the-day recorded on a telephone answering machine. "Take a Break in Your Day. Dial Daybreak. 258-7700." I could only afford one such printed t-shirt. I wore it a lot. Daybreak evolved into the Monday Morning Memo and a trilogy of best-sellers, then became the foundation upon which Wizard Academy was built. Have you visited our 22-acre campus?

7. Hand Stamps. One of my friends recently attended a ticketed event that required a hand-stamp for readmission. The hand-stamp was a delightful little mini-ad for one of the sponsors. Can you imagine a better advertising vehicle for creating personal identification with a brand? There's something about looking down at your own hand and seeing a logo and knowing that the image has value. You're having fun, the brand is there, and it's part of you. The ink might wash off, but the impression doesn't fade so quickly.

8. Publicity Stunt. Few things are as powerful as a publicity stunt that wins public attention. Going for inclusion in the Guinness Book of World Records requires a lot of work, but holding a world record is extremely cool. Did you hear about the guy who dropped a golf ball at the edge of Mongolia, then whacked it 1,234 miles all the way to the other side? The journey required 12,170 swings of the club, 90 days and 510 lost balls. But he got interviewed by Jay Leno on *The Tonight Show* followed by *The Today Show, CNN, CNN International, CTV, ESPN Cold Pizza,* and *PGA Tour Sunday.* Articles were published about him in the *New York Times* and the *Times of London.* Then the *Associated Press* issued a worldwide story about the exploit. *Outside Magazine* featured him as one of its 25 Coolest People, the *Men's Journal* put him in their Hall of Fame, *National Public Radio* broadcast their interview with him from coast to coast, then several European radio networks jumped on the bandwagon. Not a bad R.O.I. on a 90-day investment.

9. Self-Publish a Book. Nothing screams "expert" quite so loudly as writing a book on a subject. So get an ISBN number, register it with the Library of Congress, pay a printer to print your book, and then sell it on Amazon.com. You may sell only a few copies, but the copies you give away will make you a fortune. You won't make any money on the book. But you'll make a fortune *because* of the book.

10. Spray-Painted Signs. In the early 1970s, "Hamp Baker says Drive with Care" was spray-painted on car hoods salvaged from crumpled automobiles, then those hoods were tied with bailing wire to barbed-wire fences across the state. Nobody in Oklahoma had ever heard of Hamp Baker, but his name was soon a household word. When he ran for public office, he won by a landslide.

You may have noticed that each of these things requires time and creative energy. There's no one you can call to do these things for you, you've got to do them yourself. But if you're willing to spend a little time to make a lot of money, pick 1 or 2 items from the list above, then get to work.

And prepare to be amazed.

Roy H. Williams

19
Preliminary Counteraction

Preliminary Counteraction dictates that a person take steps to counteract a negative action before the negative action occurs. This lens is typically applied as follows:

1. If it will be necessary to do an action with both harmful and useful effects, this action should be replaced with anti-actions to control harmful effects.
    a. e.g. Buffer a solution to prevent harm from pH extremes
2. Create beforehand stresses in an object that will oppose known undesirable working stresses later on.
    a. e.g. Wearing a lead apron on the parts of the body not being exposed to X-rays

In other words, preliminary counteraction means that you should use anti-actions to control harmful effects.

Preheat Car Engines and Concrete Rebar

When a car is started in a very cold climate, the oil is sitting at the bottom of the pan in a near solid form. Obviously, the engine cannot run without oil. Cold starts do increase engine wear and reduce battery life. In this scenario, the negative or harmful effect is the damage caused to the automobile by a cold start. The preliminary counteraction is in the form of a preheated car engine.

A preheated car engine solves the problem by heating the oil in the pan before the car is started. Implementing a preliminary counteraction solves the problem, reducing engine wear and extending the vehicle's battery life.

In some cases, the preliminary counteraction involves leaving a seemingly negative effect in place. For example, conventional wisdom dictates that rust should be removed from the rebar before concrete is poured. That's a bad idea. The rust actually makes the bond between the rebar and the concrete stronger; so the preliminary counteraction in this situation is to leave the rust intact.

Please the Negative Nicks

Preliminary counteraction can also be applied to standard business practices. For instance, if you are preparing a proposal or presentation and you know that there is a negative manager or employer who is certain to torpedo your presentation, involve that person beforehand. Try to identify what their reaction will be ahead of time so that you can adequately prepare and avoid a showdown in the meeting.

I use the Preliminary Counteraction lens to improve my proposals. When I write a proposal, I brainstorm for an hour from the view point of my top competitor and then address the drawbacks in my proposal. Even though this section is normally not specified in the RFP (request for proposal), I review the negative aspects of the proposal beforehand.

If you know and understand your weaknesses beforehand, you will be better able to discuss how you can fix the problem and why your audience shouldn't be concerned with the issue.

TRIZ Bitz
1. Offer early retirement to employees in times of slow growth to minimize layoffs
2. Require up-and-coming employees to spend time in each business discipline to gain a wider perspective before promotion
3. Arrive one hour early for your speech to resolve any problems with room or A/V equipment

What negative or harmful effects exist in your product or service that you can rectify beforehand?

Actions Speak Louder Than

I'm a big believer in the power of words. But when words aren't backed by corresponding actions, talk is cheap.

Have you ever felt a disconnection between what a company promised you in their ads and what they actually delivered?

I carry a list of companies in my head called the "Never Again As Long As I Live" list. I'll bet you have one, too.

Was it the advertising of these companies that put them on our lists? Of course not. It was their actions.

One dumb decision can undo years of good advertising.

What decisions have you made that send signals to your customers?

"Who you are speaks so loudly I can't hear what you're saying."
— Ralph Waldo Emerson

1. What are you saying in your ads?
2. Who are you being in your store?
3. Is there a disconnect?

A dog doesn't have to growl to let me know it's dangerous. *Just bare your teeth, doggie. I'll understand.* This small, direct signal from the dog overrides all the assurances of its owner: "He won't bite, he's a friendly dog. I've had him for 10 years. His breed never bites. It's been proven. Here, watch this. See, he didn't bite me and he won't bite you either. What are you afraid of? Here are some testimonials from other people who have petted him. Did you know this dog was voted Most Pettable Dog of 2007? He won't bite you, he likes you. Trust me. We care about our customers."

What is advertising but the assurances of a dog owner?

Talk, when it costs you nothing, is cheap.

"Here are ten, hundred-dollar bills. Put them in your pocket. If this dog so much as snaps at you, they're yours. He wasn't baring his teeth to scare you. He was smiling at you."

Wow. A smiling dog. I think I'll pet him.

Actions are powerful signals when they agree with your words.

These action-signals gain credibility to the degree they cost you one or more of the following:

1. Material Wealth
2. Time & Energy
3. Opportunity
4. Power & Control
5. Reputation & Prestige
6. Safety & Well Being

What do your signals cost you? What are you risking?

Words that cost you little have little meaning.

Roy H. Williams

20
Preliminary Action

Not all preliminary steps are counteractions. Sometimes, a preliminary action is necessary to improve efficiency and make things easier for the consumer or user.

Preliminary Action is typically applied as follows:

1. Perform, before it is needed, the required change of an object (either fully or partially).
    a. i.e. Sterilizing surgical instruments on a sealed tray prior to the procedure

2. Pre-arrange objects such that they can come into action from the most convenient place and without losing time for their delivery.
    a. i.e. A flexible manufacturing cell

Simplify the Customer's Role

Perforated stamps are a preliminary action. The stamps must be separated before they can be used, and so the process is performed prior to purchase.

Pre-paid return labels are another excellent example of preliminary action. The return rate for women's apparel purchased online is almost 30%. With those odds, online clothing retailers know that the merchandise is quite likely to come back. Pre-paid return labels remove a necessary step from the return process before the action is even required. Companies that do not include pre-paid return labels with the clothes are likely to struggle because the return process is intimidating and confusing to consumers. Pre-paid return labels simplify the customer's job – and happy customers are more likely to be repeat customers.

Another application of preliminary action is the assembly of pieces by manufacturers. In the past, if you purchased a barbecue grill that required assembly, you'd open the box to find 400 pieces. Now, you might find six pieces that you snap together. The manufacturers have simplified the process by doing work ahead of time and assembling pieces to make the customer's task easier.

Anyone with a large set of tools in their garage can relate to the next example. Shadow boards are used to organize tools and keep order in the workspace. On a shadow board, the outline of the tool is painted on the board. When you finish working with the tool, all you have to do is look for the shape on the board and you'll know exactly where the object belongs.

Market research is another example of preliminary action. Marketers do their homework and learn about their customer base *before* launching an expensive marketing or advertising campaign.

Finally, a food preparation chain known in Utah as "My Girlfriend's Kitchen," (the same business model goes by different names in different states) has simplified meal preparation for busy families. When you visit the store, you select a number of recipes that you would like to prepare. All of the food is pre-chopped, laid out, and ready to go. The customer simply selects their desired meals, quickly assembles the ingredients, and takes the finished product home. The meals can then be frozen until needed. This chain makes answering the question, "What's for dinner?" a cinch.

TRIZ Bitz

1. Review location of sex offenders online before purchasing a home
2. Walt Disney's famous story-boarding technique for cartoon development
3. Modular automobile designs to allow implementation of unique customer requests

What can you do to simplify your product or process for customers? Can you take preliminary action to improve efficiency?

21
Beforehand Compensation

"So what do you think?"

"That's the stupidest thing I have ever read."

That was my first indication that I might be on the right track.

"It doesn't say what you are actually going to do."

"I know. That's the beauty of it."

Pat Riley's book, *The One Page Proposal*, is an invaluable resource that shows you how to get things done in business. He learned the secrets of the proposal from one of the richest men in the world, Adnan Khashoggi.

A One Page Proposal is a document that succinctly expresses all the facts, reasoning, and conditions surrounding an undertaking or project. A One Page Proposal uses persuasive language to build a case for approval and propose a specific course of action. A good proposal fulfills all of these specifications within a single printed page.

But sometimes a proposal can be deceptively simple.

I have used the principles in the book countless times, and even though I had never met the author, I have been plugging Pat's book for years.

So I decided that I would put together a one page proposal and send the document to Pat.

Basically, my proposal was a chopped-down version of my resume. I included an explanation that I was always looking for new ventures and partnerships. The punch line was this:

"I will work for you for 60 days on anything you want me to for free. If you want to discuss working together after that, then we will cross that bridge when we get to it. No strings attached."

How could he say no to someone who wanted to work for free?

My wife thought my idea was stupid because I didn't tell him what I wanted to work on, but how could I? I had no idea what he was working on, but I assumed he was well connected and had some interesting projects in the works.

Classic Beforehand Compensation. I removed any reason for him to say no before we ever met.

I overnighted the proposal and he called me the very next day.

We have been working on projects together ever since.

Technically, Beforehand Compensation involves preparing emergency means beforehand to compensate for the relatively low reliability of an object. Skydivers packing a backup parachute and the magnetic strip on film that directs the developer to compensate for poor exposure are both great examples; however, as you can see from my proposal story, not all beforehand compensation has to be related to the lack of reliability of an object.

I think I'm a pretty reliable guy – but Pat didn't know that yet, so I had to compensate for the fact that he had no idea what I am capable of.

Preparing for the Worst

Automobile airbags are a classic example of Beforehand Compensation. The low reliability in this system is the driver. People make mistakes, so automobile manufacturers install airbags to prevent injuries or death.

Fire extinguishers and evacuation routes are also examples of emergency means prepared in advance to counter low reliability. Natural disasters and fires are unpredictable, and certainly not reliable.

Frequently Asked Question pages on a Web site fulfill a similar purpose. Companies figure out beforehand the top 10 to 20 questions customers are likely to ask and then put the answers on the Web site where they are readily accessible.

Finally, software backup systems are designed to prepare for the worst and counter the relatively low reliability of computer systems. Remember the episode of "Sex and the City" where Carrie never backed up her computer? Without the backup programs, businesses and individuals could lose years of work to a glitch or virus.

TRIZ Bitz
1. Hurricane evacuation signs throughout Florida highways
2. Emergency board meeting to discuss lower than expected revenue for the quarter
3. Show your first event as sold-out regardless of participation to generate future interest

How do you compensate for low reliability in your business, product, or service? Can you compensate for this liability to improve your product?

22
Equipotentiality

The technical definition of equipotentiality states that in a potential field, one should limit position changes. In other words, change operating conditions to eliminate the need to raise or lower objects in a gravity field. For example: spring-loaded parts delivery system in a factory or locks in a channel between two bodies of water (think the Panama Canal).

In other words, you should eliminate the need to work against a field. Consider the altitude compensator carburetors on my airplane. They are very advanced; my carburetors adjust the air/fuel mixture automatically based on pressure using a spring and diaphragm. In most airplanes, as you change altitude, you constantly have to change the mixture of the fuel because there is less oxygen at higher altitudes.

Keep Newton's Apple Afloat

Another example is the spring lift mechanism for dinner plates at restaurant buffets. The plates are stacked on a spring that compensates for the pull of gravity. In other words, the spring works against gravity. Every time a patron removes a plate from the pile, the next plate slides back up in its place.

Grounding straps accomplish a similar objective. If you've ever worked around explosives, you'll notice that the workers' uniforms include a grounding strap to eliminate the static electricity. The straps eliminate the need to work against the field, or in this case, reduce the likelihood of static causing an explosion.

Frisbees use the gravity field to their advantage. When the Frisbee spins in the air, it creates just enough airflow to float, thus eliminating the need to raise or lower the toy in the field. The Frisbee accomplishes that on its own.

Like many of the other lenses, equipotentiality is not restricted to literal interpretation. For instance, have you ever worked for a business where you can never reach the decision-maker because there are too many levels in the organization? These levels are working against the field, or the gravity, of being able to get to the decision-maker. Making the organization "flatter" could solve the problem.

As you can see, liberal definitions of the lenses are often necessary to uncover the greater potential for each principle. Don't be afraid to "think outside the box" and springboard off of these lenses to come up with your own solution or idea.

TRIZ Bitz
1. Use a magnetic field to protect astronauts from space radiation on their trip to Mars
2. Falkirk rotating boat lift in Scotland that connects two canals at different elevations
3. Maglevs (Magnetically levitated trains)

How can you eliminate the need to work against gravity in your business? How can you make your product or service "flatter" or more level?

Are Your Ads Getting Enough Complaints?

When an ad campaign is producing big results, there will usually be complaints from the public.

When an ad campaign is getting poor results, the public rarely complains.

What makes people hate an ad?

1. It's hard to ignore.
Any ad that makes its point sharply will be an irritant.
But sharp-pointed ads are also the most effective.

2. It presents a tightly focused perspective.
Any ad that makes assumptions about the experiences of the customer will be judged as presumptive. Persons whose experiences are otherwise usually hate these ads.
But presumptive ads connect powerfully to customers whose personal experiences are accurately mirrored in the ad.

3. It's given a lot of repetition.
There is such a thing as too much repetition. And the sharper the ad's point, the less repetition will be required. *But "too much repetition" is often the charge that's leveled against an ad that's annoying for reasons 1 or 2.*

"Hello, I'm a Mac."
"And I'm a PC."

Very few people are ambiguous about the "Get a Mac" TV campaign:

"Apple's mean-spirited new ad campaign... Ad Report Card Grade: C+... And isn't smug superiority, no matter how affable and casually dressed, a bit off-putting as a brand strategy?"
– Seth Stevenson

"I don't know about you but I have had about enough of those Mac TV commercials that consistently rip on Microsoft and the PC. Any company that needs to badmouth the competition in an effort to sell their product is a company I don't want anything to do with."
– ElectroGeek

"The *Los Angeles Times* has a big article for you about Justin Long, aka the Mac from the 'Get a Mac' ads… [The article goes on to explain that Justin Long is a 'smug little twit.'] Also of note: There are apparently 20 more of these ads in the can, ensuring that everyone will be sick of them eventually."

– Tim Nudd

"Reporting a $546 million profit on Wednesday, Apple also said that it shipped over 1.6 million Macs representing over 30 percent growth from the year-ago quarter. According to Apple CFO Peter Oppenheimer, this represents the strongest quarter in the company's history."

– Jim Dalrymple, reporter

Complain about me all you want. Just leave the 546 million with my butler at the front door.

Are your ads getting complaints? If not, why not?
A: Do you have no sharp points to make?
B: Or are you just afraid to make them?

Turn the poles of a magnet North to South and CLICK, they connect. Turn the poles North to North and they'll repel each other just as powerfully. Advertising, like a magnet, is subject to the Law of Polarity: *Your ad's ability to attract customers cannot exceed its potential to repel.*

Most ads aren't written to make a point sharply. They're written not to offend.

How are your ads written?

Roy H. Williams

23
The Other Way Round

Usually, the lens of The Other Way Round is applied as follows:

1. Invert the action used to solve the problem.
    a. i.e. Instead of cooling an object, heat it

2. Make movable parts (or the external environment) fixed and fixed parts moveable.
    a. i.e. A moving sidewalk with standing people

3. Turn the object or process upside down.
    a. i.e. Turn an assembly upside down to insert fasteners

Basically, The Other Way Round suggests that you should do the opposite of what you've been doing or invert the action.

There are many examples of this principle. If you lived in a community inundated with fast-food restaurants, a smart business plan might be to open up a "slow-food" restaurant to differentiate yourself from the competition. Do the opposite of what everyone else is doing and you'll stand out from the crowd.

You could also benchmark yourself against the worst, rather than the best in your field. Compare your business to the worst company in the industry and discover all the ways *not* to do things so that you don't do them. Again, do the opposite.

If you commute to work, see if you can't work from home. Tired of cleaning the artwork indentations on a wood chopping board? Why not just flip the board over? The opposite surface is smooth and easy to clean.

Isn't this easy? Of course, The Other Way Round can also be applied to very complex issues.

Searching for the Needle

Kary Mullis, a student of Wizard Academy, won the 1993 Nobel Prize in Chemistry for his development of the Polymerase Chain Reaction (PCR). PCR is a cornerstone of biochemistry and molecular biology because the technology allows for the amplification of DNA sequences. A great deal of Kary's work revolves around the principle of doing things "The Other Way Round."

While everyone else in the world was trying to find the figurative needle in the haystack and chemically find and hold DNA, Kary decided to let the DNA replicate itself instead. Rather than looking for the needle in the haystack, Kary let the needle reproduce itself billions and billions of times so that the DNA was easier to find and capture.

By doing things The Other Way Round, Dr. Mullis received the highest honors in his field.

In fact, Dr. Mullis is currently doing research on how to counter bio-terrorist attacks by using the same principle – the Other Way Round. I can't tell you any more than that right now because it is a highly secret program.

All I can say is that Roy and I are certain he will win another Nobel Prize for his work.

TRIZ Bitz

1. Start writing your novel in the middle of the story
2. Clock faces where the numbers go backwards
3. High heel women's shoe where the heel is horizontal off of the front of the shoe instead of vertical off the heel

What can you do with your business, product, or service by doing the opposite of what everyone else is doing?

24
Curvature

The lens of Curvature is typically applied in one of three ways:

1. Instead of using rectilinear parts, surfaces, or forms, use curvilinear ones; move from flat surfaces to spherical ones; from parts shaped as a cube to ball-shaped structures.
   a. i.e. Use arches and domes for strength in architecture

2. Use rollers, balls, spirals, domes.
   a. i.e. Ballpoint and roller point pens for smooth ink distribution

3. Go from linear to rotary motion, use centrifugal forces.
   a. i.e. Rather than wringing clothes to remove the water, spin the clothes in a washing machine instead

Curvature can be used to improve the design or efficiency of a product.

Furniture, Film, and Ferraris

For instance, think about the spherical casters on a couch, rolling chair, or shopping cart. A castor (or caster) is a type of wheel that is mounted with a steering pivot. A bearing above the wheel allows the wheel to rotate 360 degrees and automatically swivel to align the load in the direction in which the object is being pushed. The curvature design of the castor makes pushing, rotating, and turning large loads much easier.

Camera film is another example of improved efficiency and design via the principle of curvature. Photographers used to have to carry photographic film plates with them to capture their snapshots. Then the film design and material was changed so that it could be curved and rolled into carrying cases. The new plastic film allowed photographers to capture multiple images on one roll of film, rather than carrying 40 or more film plates with them to each shoot.

Automobile designers use the principle of curvature to improve design. The curved angles and edges of cars are greatly preferred by consumers to the former box-style designs that dominated the roadways. Curvature is a big selling point for car manufacturers.

I continue to encourage you to use liberal definitions of the lenses. How about the opposite of curvature? Have you noticed how Toyota and Honda have brought back the cute, boxy shape cars recently?

Much like the other lenses, curvature does not have to be applied literally. Curvature can be used in terms of "throwing a curve" at your team. For instance, I knew a manager at Thiokol who used to throw curve balls at his team every once in a while to keep them on their toes. This manager would announce role changes during regular staff meetings. He would place the Head of Engineering in charge of Quality; make the Development Manager in charge of Operations; and so on. He would just flip everyone around to throw a curve at them and make them learn something completely different.

His team was constantly learning new skills and gaining command of different aspects of the business because he threw enough curves to keep them sharp.

TRIZ Bitz

1. Use curved, pleasing lines in your Web site design instead of rectangular lines
2. Dr. Scholl's shoe inserts with multiple foot arch designs
3. Seats arranged in a curve around the presentation screen so no one has to twist their necks to see

How could you use the lens of curvature to improve your product or team's design or efficiency?

25
Dynamics

The lens of dynamics involves changing the static design of a product, system, or service. This principle is usually applied as follows:

1. Allow or design the characteristics of an object, external environment, or process to change to be optimal or to find an optimal operating condition.
    a. i.e. Adjustable steering wheels, seats, and mirror positions

2. Divide an object into parts capable of movement relative to each other.
    a. i.e. The "butterfly" computer keyboard

3. If an object or process is rigid or inflexible, make it movable or adaptive.
    a. i.e. A flexible boroscope for examining engines

Changing the Dynamic

In other words, the principle of Dynamics means you allow the part to change or have relative movement. Think about self-breaking street lamp poles. When a car hits one of the poles, the pole breaks away from the base, rather than damaging the car and injuring the passengers. These street poles have been designed to allow relative movement.

In an earthquake zone, buildings are designed with springs so that they can move with the shaking earth. The building's structure allows for mobility, which helps absorb the shock in a quake.

The dictionary defines dynamic as *characterized by continuous change, activity, or progress; of or relating to energy or to objects in motion.*

Can you think of another instance of a changing object?

What about the toolbar on your computer? You can move the icons and options around to customize the toolbar to best suit your needs. The toolbar is ever-changing, and has relative movement in relation to the user's needs.

Freeway delay status signs are another great example. As you're driving down the road, the signs are updated to reflect delays on busy highways and interstates, i.e. "Fifteen minutes to I-35." The signs change because traffic is dynamic and always changing. A static status message would be of little use to drivers because the information would always be dated and irrelevant.

One final example is a new technology that allows advertisers to shine images on the side of a building. The dynamic aspect of the technology lies in the owner's ability to change the advertising on the fly. The ad is projected on the building by a software program and a projector. One click of the mouse and, bam! Ad changed.

TRIZ Bitz
1. Automatic rebalancing of internal holding within your 401K once a year
2. Digital picture frame
3. Billboard where the faces follow you as you walk by

How can you change your product or service to allow for relative movement? Can your product be modified so that the user can customize its function for optimal operating conditions?

26
Partial or Excessive Action

"I am not going to sign it."

"What? You have to."

"No I don't."

"Yes you do, it's the company policy."

I was buying lunch at Taco Bell when I found myself grappling with the kid at the counter. He was demanding that I sign the Visa card slip for $2.39. I didn't see the need for my signature.

He continued to state his case, that it was a requirement that all customers sign the credit card slip to complete the transaction.

I pointed to the drive-thru window.

"How come when I drove through there last week I didn't have to sign anything?"

"The drive-thru is different."

"Why is it different? I don't think my Visa card knows the difference."

"I don't know. That's just our policy."

"Well your policy doesn't make sense. I assumed you guys

got smart enough to not require signatures at the drive-thru so that you can move more customers through faster. Right? More customers per hour equal more revenue. So why don't you apply that same logic here at the counter?"

"Listen Mister, I just work here."

I started to tear into him about how he should take some initiative and question management on the policy. I was getting ready to tell him that speaking up might lead to a promotion when the Harley biker behind me said something about five seconds and sticking that card slip where the sun doesn't shine if I didn't move along.

I shut up, but my point was valid. The credit card slip was a perfect example of the principle of Partial or Excessive Actions.

Technically speaking, the lens of Partial or Excessive Actions is defined as follows:

If 100% of an objective is hard to achieve using a given solution method, then by using "slightly less" or "slightly more" of the same method, the problem may be considerably easier to solve.

For instance, you "top off" your tank when you fill up at the gas station.

By doing slightly more or less, you can solve your problem more easily and efficiently.

Think about a stencil mat for a moment. When you are spray painting a design using the stencil, you're going to use **more** paint than you would have if you'd just painted on the designs. Even though you're over spraying, the process is much faster with the mat.

Exceeding Expectations

Many companies apply this lens to their customer service process. Word-of-mouth marketing is a "free" marketing tool that companies can employ to spread the word about their businesses reputation, but beware, because word-of-mouth marketing can backfire.

Customers are far more likely to share a bad experience with their friends than to speak highly of their experience. If customers have a bad experience with your company, they will tell everyone they know. If they have an average or expected experience, they are unlikely to mention your business at all.

However, if you can *greatly exceed* the customer's expectations and go above and beyond to make their experience with your company positive, they will share their good experience with their friends.

Companies have to go far beyond what their customers expect to make word-of-mouth marketing a viable resource. An average experience will generate zero results. Only by adding **more** to the customer service process can companies achieve stellar results, but you have to go far beyond what is expected.

Less Can Be More

The Taco Bell story at the beginning of the chapter is a great example of a time when less is more. It took retail years to figure out that speeding up the transaction for smaller purchases makes way more sense. Sure, the risk goes up slightly for the merchant in the event of a dispute because the customer didn't sign the stupid little piece of paper, but how many people are going to dispute 2 bucks anyway?

Eliminating the signature process for small purchases is the simplest case of risk management I can think of, balancing the risk versus the reward. Micromanaging, or adding more to the process, doesn't do anything to improve efficiency or satisfaction in most cases.

Less is more. If you have to create rough illustrations for a project, sketching the images is much quicker and easier than drawing each picture in detail. Sketching uses less effort, and for a preliminary draft, accomplishes basically the same result.

TRIZ Bitz
1. Prevention of a riot by showing excessive police force
2. African Americans fighting for more rights by less fighting back
3. Slightly less movement in your backswing to improve control

What can you add or subtract from your product or service to improve the end result? How could you improve operations in your business by using **a little less or a little more?**

27
Another Dimension

Another Dimension can be defined according to four principles:

1. To move an object in two- or three- dimensional space.
   a. i.e. An infrared computer mouse moves in space during presentations, rather than on a flat surface

2. Use multi-story arrangement of objects rather than a single-story arrangement.
   a. i.e. Replace a cassette with six CDs to increase music time and variety

3. Tilt or reorient the object; lay the object on its side.
   a. i.e. A dump truck
   b. Baja Beer (liberal definitions of the lenses allows for all kinds of overlap; this is a good thing)

4. Use "another side" of a given area.
   a. i.e. Stack microelectric hybrid circuits to improve density

An Alternate Aspect

Think about an IMAX movie. What dimension does the film play in? The images are not two-dimensional or three-dimensional; they are in another dimension all together. The surround sound and gigantic screen create a new world for viewers.

Disney World uses "another dimension" to keep up illusions.

The theme park has underground tunnels that the staff uses to take out trash and move around the park when they are out of costume. There is a whole underground network at Disney – another dimension used to move people and equipment around.

Microbreweries in a restaurant or bar operate on a similar principle, yet in an opposite manner. Rather than hiding the inner mechanisms of the system, the breweries display their HVAC systems for customers to look at. By revealing the machinery, the owners have changed the actual dimension and layout of the building's structure. Rather than putting the "other dimension" underground or out of sight, they reveal this new dimension to the customers for their viewing pleasure.

Finally, Toronto's CN Tower, the world's tallest building, reveals another dimension to visitors. The building has a glass floor that is 330 feet in the air. Looking through this floor to see the world alters the viewer's perspective and dimensions.

Did the new Grand Canyon Skywalk attraction snowball on this idea? If you haven't seen it, there is a new horseshoe shaped walk with glass floors that overhangs the Grand Canyon.

I am certain, however, they never used the full power of Sensible Design when they created their business. You experience this beautiful view (that you pay good money for) but they won't let you take any pictures!

TRIZ Bitz
1. A water park slide with a clear tube that goes through a shark tank
2. Actively participating in the online virtual world of Second Life
3. Using hypnosis to cure ailments

Can you reorient, stack, tilt, move, or use another side of your product or service to achieve another dimension? How could you change your product or service to reveal (or hide) another dimension?

Can You Make It Talk?
People are more interesting than non-people.

Mingle a bit of wood, paint and cloth, then drench the pile in sparkling imagination and a new person leaps onto the stage.

Few techniques in communication are as powerful – or as often overlooked – as personification: *ascribing human characteristics to inanimate objects.*

It turns dead corporate brands into living persons. Who are the Keebler Elves, the Jolly Green Giant, Mr. Clean and Ronald McDonald if not *personifications* of the brands they represent?

This memo isn't about clumsy corporate cartoon characters. Personification is much bigger and more elegant than mere mascots and logos. When conceived in words, lively words, personification summons the imagination and triggers the emotions.

Listen to how Robert Frost gives human characteristics to inanimate objects in his storm poem, *Once by the Pacific:*

The shattered water made a misty din.
Great waves looked over others coming in,
And thought of doing something to the shore
That water never did to land before.
The clouds were low and hairy in the skies,
Like locks blown forward in the gleam of eyes.
You could not tell, and yet it looked as if
The shore was lucky in being backed by cliff,
The cliff in being backed by continent;
It looked as if a night of dark intent
Was coming, and not only a night, an age.
Someone had better be prepared for rage.
There would be more than ocean-water broken
Before God's last 'Put out the Light' was spoken.

Waves **looked over** others and **thought** of doing something to the shore, which **was lucky** in being backed by cliff?

Personification. Can you do it? Can you speak a person into existence?

Herman Melville did it 156 years ago in 3 short words, "Call me Ishmael."

215

I did it 12 years ago in 5 words for Rolex and Everest, "...the world's most angry mountain."

Apple is doing it in 7 words right now. "I'm a Mac." "And I'm a PC." (Did it ever occur to you that the audio track from these ads would work even better on radio than it does on TV? Evidently, it's never occurred to anyone who sells radio airtime, either.)

We gaze longer at pictures that have people in them than at pictures that have no people. I believe the same is true of words. We pay more attention to words that tell us of people than to words that don't.

That's enough rambling for one Monday morning. Now go look Today in the eyes, smile sweetly and say, "I own you. You're mine. You're happy and warm and comforting and good and if you think for one second that I'm going to let you be otherwise, you're sadly mistaken."

Be firm. Days can become unruly if you let them.

Roy H. Williams

28
Mechanical Vibration

I popped in the VHS tape and flopped on the couch next to Barbara.

"OK. Now watch how easily the wings come off."

An older couple, probably in their late 60s, was removing the wings from the Pulsar with the greatest of ease, all the while smiling happily at the camera.

We were watching a promotional video for a new experimental airplane called the Pulsar XP. I had recently gotten my pilot's license and like most people, could not afford to buy an airplane of my own. Not being mechanically inclined was certainly a drawback, but I was strongly considering buying an experimental airplane kit and building one myself. Building the craft myself was the only plausible economic answer to my desire for a plane of my own.

"See how easily the wings come off? Those two *blue hairs* can do it; no problem. If the wings can come off that easily, then I won't even need a hangar for the airplane. I can just store it in the garage."

Barbara wasn't really buying the whole dog and pony show, but she finally gave me the OK to buy the kit.

About 1,300 beers later, tail number N96MF finally went *wheels up*.

Even with my first flight jitters, I managed to survive; yours truly, crash helmet, and plane all intact.

The wing removal was another story. The manufacturer recommends that you remove the wings several times during flight testing for inspection to make sure everything is A –OK, so I had to perform this act of hell several times.

I am not sure what magical powers the couple on the video possessed, but those wings took many days, lots of friends, and lots of blood to get them to *turn loose*. The tightness of the pins that held them in place made them nearly impossible to remove. The airplane designer could have taken a lesson from ship hinge pins.

It took months before I found the right shake.

I spent many hours on the tip of the wing trying to vibrate it at various shakes, rattles and rolls, while a friend pulled on the connection pins. Finally, I learned the right  dance with the wing tip that allows the pins to be removed without any blood. To this day I cannot explain my special moves well enough to tell someone else how to remove the wings with ease, but I found the magic. The problem was fixed with the perfect vibration.

Technically speaking, mechanical vibration is usually applied as follows:

1. Cause an object to oscillate or vibrate.
    a. i.e. An electric carving knife with vibrating blades

2. Increase the object's frequency, even up to the ultrasonic.
    a. i.e. Distribute powder with vibration

3. Use an object's resonant frequency.
   a. i.e. Destroy gall or kidney stones using ultrasonic resonance

4. Use piezoelectric vibrators in place of mechanical ones.
   a. i.e. Quartz crystal oscillations drive high accuracy clocks

5. Use combined ultrasonic and electromagnetic field oscillations.
   a. i.e. Mixing alloys in an induction furnace

Shake Things Up

Everything vibrates and has its own unique natural frequency. Vibration can often be the solution to your problem. Change the frequency, amplitude, period, or cycle, experiment, and see what happens.

Washing machines vibrate during the wash cycle to help break up the dirt on fabrics. Cell phones vibrate to silently (in theory) notify the owner of an incoming call.

Mechanical Vibration does not always require literal physical movement. For instance, an organization might "shake things up" and change the company's management, systems, and processes to achieve better productivity and profit.

Eyeballs and Astronauts

Sometimes your goal is to remove the vibration. Upon the landing of the first Space Shuttle launch, the astronauts went through an extensive debriefing. One of their complaints was particularly odd.

They said during the first two minutes of the ascent, they had a very hard time seeing; everything was blurred. Then, as soon as the Solid Rocket Boosters separated, everything was OK. How could the SRBs cause the pilots' vision to blur?

Upon investigation we found that the human eye has a natural frequency between one and two hertz. Sure enough, when we looked at earlier rocket test data, we saw that the SRBs generated a vibration that registered exactly in this range.

We had to make a modification to the boosters to minimize this frequency in this range.

Everything vibrates.

Have you ever been driving down the road and rolled the windows down only to suddenly notice a very awkward feeling in your inner ear? The wind and pressure swirling around that exact configuration has stimulated the natural frequency of your ear drum.

TRIZ Bitz
1. Panning for gold
2. Coin-operated massage chairs in airports
3. Animals serve as a warning when they run due to vibrations caused by an oncoming tsunami

Can you shake up your product, system, or service to improve efficiency?

29
Periodic Action

The principle of Periodic Action is exactly as it sounds. This lens involves taking action in increments to improve efficiency. The principle is usually applied as follows:

1. Instead of continuous action, use periodic or pulsating actions.
   a. i.e. Hitting a nail with a hammer

2. If an action is already periodic, change the periodic magnitude or frequency.
   a. i.e. Replace a continuous siren sound with an alarm that changes in amplitude and frequency

3. Use pauses between impulses to perform a different action.
   a. i.e. In cardiopulmonary respiration (CPR), breathe after every five chest compressions

In other words, you look at your problem, business, or product through this lens to determine whether a change in the action or a segmentation of the action will improve the product.

For example, random drug testing is more efficient than scheduled drug test dates because employees will have no way to anticipate for or prepare to pass the screening. If the dates were scheduled in advance or occurred with regular frequency, employees could plan their drug use around the set dates or take cleansing pills at an appropriate time before the screen.

The siren example above is a perfect example of periodic action. If you watch an old episode of Mayberry RFD, you'll hear the sirens emitting a constant whine. The sirens of today vary in frequency and amplitude to alert citizens of danger. The periodic change in sound makes the alert more noticeable.

Sabbaticals, Software, and Siestas

Sabbaticals are another example of periodic action. A sabbatical is a hiatus from the work routine designed to allow the employee, typically a professor, scientist, or physician, an opportunity to fulfill a personal goal such as writing a book or completing an extensive research project. The sabbatical is a career break taken in periodic increments.

Some computers rely on software programs to take periodic action to scan for viruses or defragment the hard drive. The equipment can be scheduled to run periodically, typically at night when electric rates are reduced and the user doesn't need to be using the computer for other tasks.

A siesta is also a periodic action. Rather than going to sleep for an extended period of time, a person can take a short nap to improve their alertness and efficiency.

TRIZ Bitz

1. Tapping into unused PC computing power while people are asleep
2. Eliminating verbal pauses through Toastmaster training
3. Politicians periodically stopping to think about their actions

Can you use periodic actions to improve the efficiency of your product or service?

30
Continuity of Useful Action

Continuity of Useful Action essentially means working at full capacity and eliminating idle time. This lens is usually applied in one of two ways:

1. Carry on work continuously; make all parts of an object work at full load, all the time.
   a. i.e. A flywheel or hydraulic system stores energy when a vehicle stops so that the motor can continue running at optimum power

2. Eliminate all idle or intermittent actions or work.
   a. i.e. Print during the printer carriage's return

Busy Bees

In some ways, Continuity of Useful Action is similar to multitasking. For instance, if you listen to an audio book while driving, you are using that time efficiently and eliminating idle time.

A 24-hour mechanic is another great application of this lens. Rather than having the shop sit empty for 12 hours a day, a 24-hour mechanic makes full use of all the hours in the day and available resources. There is no idle time; the mechanics are carrying on with their work continuously.

On a similar note, I've often wondered why restaurants offer different menus at different times. Why not just offer all of the items at all times? The ingredients and resources are already available, so why not use them? Making the entire menu available at all times keeps the kitchen working at full capacity.

The military has Continuity of Useful Action down to an exact science. Anyone who has been in the military knows that there is no idle time. Every minute, every hour, of every day, is put to good use (or at least they tell you it's good for you). The military keeps its units running at full capacity at all times. If for some reason a soldier finds a spare moment where they have nothing to do, their commander will quickly find a task to occupy the time.

TRIZ Bitz
1. A hybrid car uses the continuous motor operation at idle to charge batteries
2. Read a poem everyday to improve your writing skills
3. An alarm clock that continues to increase in volume until shut off

Is your business running at full capacity? How could you improve the Continuity of Useful Action in your system?

31
Skipping

In Vince Poscente's book, *The Age of Speed*, he has a chapter called "Smelling the Roses" that starts as follows:

> *Using speed to live a more meaningful life is counterintuitive for most people, because speeding up means compromising the journey, missing out on smelling the roses, right? Well not necessarily. Although this is true in some scenarios, not every experience holds deep intrinsic value. Not every experience presents us with an opportunity to develop ourselves, to make deeper connections, to find meaning. And when I suggest you embrace speed, I'm not recommending faster strolls on the beach or accelerated games of catch with your child. I'm suggesting that you seek to speed up the minutiae in your work and life.*

I couldn't agree more.

Speeding up the unpleasant tasks of our life is desirable because we then free up more time to do the things we like.

One of my greatest pleasures in life was the time I spent with my Black Lab/German Shepherd mix, Lechien. As she got older, Lechien had problems with arthritis in her spine and other issues. That was a sad time, but when she got a tumor in her spleen, we had to do surgery to remove the growth.

My veterinarian, Dr. Kate, explained our options. She said, "I can do the surgery myself. I am very confident in my surgical skills. But I know a surgeon who is the best in the country, Dr. Morgan. His skills are simply the best, but more importantly, he can do the procedure in half the time it will take me. Going faster does not mean lower quality; in fact, the quality will probably be better than mine. In this case speed is on our side, because the longer she is under the anesthesia the more risk we have of her not coming out of it. Speed here is good. Dr. Morgan will cost a bit more, but the decision is yours."

My decision was clear; money didn't matter when it came to my best friend. However, Dr. Morgan's name rang a bell.

"Is Dr. Morgan's first name Paul?" I asked.

"Yes, how did you know that?"

"Well, he is actually a friend of mine."

The Universal Network strikes again.

In terms of TRIZ, Skipping is defined as "conducting a process or certain stages (usually destructible, harmful, or hazardous operations) at high speed." For instance, dentists use a high-speed drill to avoid heating their patient's periodontal tissues.

Other physicians use medical injection guns. This tool allows the doctor to "skip" over the hazardous process of injecting something into you. They're making the injections at high speed, using a highly-pressurized tool to inject medicine into your skin. This enables them to inject the medicine rapidly without making a hole or mark in your arm.

Plastic pipe cutting works on the same principle. When you cut PVC pipes, you want to slice into them very quickly with a high-speed blade or a water cutter so that the plastic isn't melted on the ends, resulting in a cleaner cut.

Scan Me, Please

I know the day is coming when you will be able to visit the grocery store, fill up your cart to the rim, and simply walk to your car without passing a cashier or the self checkout lane. A technology known as Radio-Frequency Identification allows for the automatic identification of a product from several meters away. An RFID tag can be applied to or built into a product, animal, or person.

With RFID tags for every product just around the corner, isn't it obvious that at some point we will be able to push the cart through an exit door with a built-in scanner that reads the RFID tags in the cart and then charges your credit card? Won't that be sweet?

Why not speed up the things that have no value to you or your business? Do you really like to stand in line? Do you like the quality time you spend with your dentist? Don't you love it when you spend more time at the gate than the actual flight takes?

TRIZ Bitz

1. Stop stressing over the daily value of your 401K, it's a long-term investment
2. Is this argument really going to matter tomorrow?
3. Skip worrying about what everyone thinks about you

What can you speed up or "skip" in your product or service to improve quality and efficiency?

32
Blessing in Disguise

Blessing in Disguise is typically applied as follows:

1. Use harmful factors (particularly, harmful effects of the environment or surroundings) to achieve a positive effect.
   a. i.e. Use waste heat to generate electric power

2. Eliminate the primary harmful action by adding it to another harmful action to resolve the problem.
   a. i.e. Add a buffering material to a corrosive solution

3. Amplify a harmful factor to such a degree that it is no longer harmful.
   a. i.e. Use a backfire to eliminate the fuel from a forest fire

Blessing in Disguise is essentially the idea of turning lemons into lemonade. How can you make a negative factor into a positive one?

For instance, some entrepreneurial motor heads have learned that they can use leftover cooking oil from restaurants as a fuel to power their car's engine. They're essentially taking a waste product and turning it into a valuable resource. Or think about singing the blues. Some of the greatest recording artists of our time have taken a bad scenario and made their experiences into a hit record.

Another example is computer virus attacks or firewall breaches. When a hacker breaks into your company's Web site, how do you turn that into a blessing in disguise? One great idea is to go hire the people. I've actually worked for firms that did just that. Some hacker would break into the firewall and figure out something we didn't know. Rather than getting angry, we decided to use their knowledge to our advantage and made them a part of our team.

Breakfast with the Birds

My wife and I recently took a trip to Australia. One of the stops on our trip was Port Douglas, a small town in Far North Queensland. Port Douglas has beautiful beaches that are really remote and pristine. On our first morning at the hotel, we asked the concierge, "What are some of the more popular things people do while they are here?"

The concierge immediately suggested Breakfast with the Birds, a popular tourist attraction in the region. The program sounded like a unique concept, so we decided to give it a go.

The concept sounds kind of weird, but the breakfast was actually pretty cool. They had a breakfast buffet set up outside with a canopy suspended over the eating area. All these different species of birds were allowed to walk around on the ground underneath (and sometimes on) the tables. When you're finished eating, you get to wander around the rest of the habitat, and feed and pet the kangaroos. Getting up close and personal with exotic species of birds was a really neat experience, and a very unique idea.

When the founders initially came up with their concept, they were most likely trying to figure out how to keep the birds away from the food. Birds flying overhead and dropping you know what on the customers' plates was not on the agenda. So they thought, "How can we make this work?"

That's a question you should always ask yourself. "What would it take to make this idea work?"

The founders ultimately ended up designing the canopy over the eating area so that most of the bird species cannot fly over the tables. Rather than viewing the birds as an obstacle to their plan, they turned lemons into lemonade and made the birds a key selling point of their product. The birds were, in fact, a blessing in disguise. The owners of Breakfast with the Birds took available resources and applied them much more effectively.

We had also included a Rainforest Safari on our Australia itinerary. The Safari had caught our attention because of the way the trip was advertised: small groups only. The Safari's Web site promised that there would never be more than four people on the tour.

David Armbrust, the founder of Rainforest Safari and our tour guide, arrived at the hotel on the day of our trip and picked us up in his Jeep. I quickly realized that the group size restriction is primarily in effect because David can only pick up four people in his Jeep!

David drove us about 40 minutes up into the mountains and into the rainforest. Sure enough, once we got out of the Jeep, kangaroos, wallabies, and exotic birds approached our group in search of the treats David had tucked in a pouch around his waist.

As we stood there, watching David distribute sweet potato and peanut snacks to all of the animals, a question dawned on me. I asked David, "How do you have access to the rainforest?"

He informed me that he owned the piece of land, and said, "Well, this is basically my house."

This guy picks you up in his Jeep and takes you to his backyard. He used all of his available resources, things that he already owned, to start his own business.

I asked David how long he had been feeding the animals, and he told me he'd been doing it every day for the last 20 years.

I said, "OK, so you were already feeding the animals, when one day it occurred to you to bring people along for the ride and charge them $250 a piece?"

David just smiled.

He's booked about five days a week on this Safari Tour by using his available resources and applying them more efficiently and effectively.

Look at all the available resources you have in your business. Some of these resources might seem kind of invisible at first, but you already have all kinds of resources that you can use more effectively to market your product better or to provide a better product or service.

TRIZ Bitz

1. What great things are going to happen when gasoline reaches $10 gallon? How can your business capitalize on the price of fuel?
2. When someone gets laid off from their job, aren't they almost always happier with the next one?
3. Remember Viagra? They could have scrapped the pill when it failed as a medication for hypertension.

Available resources. How can you best use them? Can you make lemons from lemonade in your business?

Do Good Ideas Always Work?

The mind is full of clever ideas. But few of them will actually work.

My friend John Young says, "A smart man makes a mistake, learns from it, and never makes that mistake again. A wise man *finds a smart man* and learns from him how to avoid that mistake altogether."

But not everyone who makes a mistake gains useful knowledge from the experience. The average person explains away their failure, forever unwilling to stare into the light and see that their sacred cow was just a cow.

Are you strong enough to see the truth and name it? Are you willing to identify the substance of your own mistakes? This humility is the key to progress.

This week a man told me the story of Betty Crocker cake mixes, the kind of story that marketing people love to tell: "Betty Crocker failed at first because all you had to do was add milk. Women didn't buy it because they felt they would be cheating their families. So the company took the powdered egg out of the mix. Then, when women had to add both milk *and* egg, they felt like they were 'cooking' and the product began to sell."

That person you see at the back of the room is me, holding up a little sign that says, "Piffle and Pooh."

Assuming that the basic facts are true, what probably happened is that the original mix produced a bad cake; powdered eggs are never as good as real ones. The explanation that "women didn't feel like they were baking" is a romantic misinterpretation of the data.

People make these excuses because it's hard to say, "Our product fell below the customer's expectations." It's easier to say, "We ran into unforeseeable circumstances." A cardboard weasel will go so far as to paint his failure the color of success by claiming, "we were ahead of our time."

The problem with making excuses is that we convince ourselves they're true, and in so doing, learn nothing. What we might have learned from the mistake is lost forever, buried under a pile of lies. And now history must repeat itself one more time.

The weasel who announced the cake mix failed because "women are mysterious creatures" was not the last of his breed. This tendency to save face is why so few people who hold a job for ten years get ten years of experience. The average blame-shifter gets one year's experience ten times. Don't let this be you.

To learn things most people will never know, you must:

1. Summon courage
2. See clearly
3. Swallow your pride
4. Speak the truth

And be sure to run with the pacesetters, the risk-takers, the possibility thinkers, people who will try what's never been done, hitters who keep their eye on the ball.

And never forget: Stay at the plate until you get a hit. You're not out until you quit trying. (The three-strike rule applies only to baseball. This is the game of life.)

I've got a bat that will fit your hands perfectly.
Think you can find your way to Wizard Academy?

See you soon.

Roy H. Williams

33
Feedback

The Feedback lens is technically applied as follows:

1. Introduce feedback (referring back, cross-checking) to improve a process or action.
   a. i.e. Automatic volume control in audio circuits

2. If feedback is already used, change its magnitude or influence.
   a. i.e. Change the sensitivity of an autopilot when the craft is within five miles of an airport

Anti-skid brakes, heart-rate monitors, quality control systems, and prototypes are all relatively straightforward examples of feedback. These systems relate the necessary data straight to the user (or the machine) so that necessary adjustments can be made instantly.

Another way to think about feedback is to consider a computer hard drive. Feedback information is included on the CD or startup disk that comes with the computer. There is a great deal of data on the hard drive that gives feedback to the head of the drive so the computer knows where the data is on the disk.

When the drive is spinning around at incredibly fast RPMs, the computer needs to know where the data is actually located so that the computer can locate the relevant information as necessary.

Straight From the Horse's Mouth

We had spent millions on promotional incentives, endcap displays, and "Spiffs" for the customer service representatives at Circuit City. We were in the middle of the Christmas rush and Iomega sales were not where they needed to be.

Our marketing department had made a big effort to get the sales representatives on the floor to sell more Zip drives. They used cash incentives, clever endcap displays, and signage galore; basically, they had done everything in their power. Or at least they thought they had.

As part of the campaign, I had volunteered to spend days, nights, and weekends on the sales floor talking to potential customers and trying to help sell our products alongside the Circuit City reps.

I couldn't figure out why we were having so much difficulty selling more products, especially considering the additional marketing collateral and incentives for the sales reps. On a hunch, I took the store manager to lunch.

"So be honest with me. Why do you think we can't sell more Zip Drives? Are the incentives we put out not attractive enough? Are the endcaps wrong? Is our message missing the target audience? Go ahead, give it to me straight. What do you think is wrong?"

After much hemming and hawing from the 23-year-old manager, I finally got him right where I wanted him. He was about to commit a cardinal sin. I could see it in his eyes; *he was going to tell me ... the truth.*

"OK....you can't tell anyone this or they will can my ass. Do you really want to know what determines which products we push?"

"Of course I do! What's the secret? Somebody gives you more money, right? Kickbacks or something like that?"

"No, it's not that at all. It's well…umm…."

"Go on …, " I prodded gently.

"OK here's the deal; we simply look at the computer reports on our PCs every morning and see what is **selling in the East coast stores**. Since we are on the West coast, we can see what is working in the Eastern Time zone before we even open. Knowing what's hot beforehand makes our lives easier because we only push those products. The hot items sell fast and easy for us.

"We make commissions on everything we sell, so we make more money selling more volume. The incentives you manufacturers give us are all about the same, so they don't really motivate us."

"Really? You base your decisions on what to push by just looking at what stores on the East coast are doing?"

"Yeah, it's pretty much that simple."

Armed with this incredible feedback, I surmised that if the company spent a lot more of our marketing dollars targeting the East coast stores, we would be better positioned to drive up the company's overall sales.

I presented my findings to Marketing. Of course, I was totally ignored.

Granted, this feedback was from just one store manager, but he had told me that all stores operate pretty much the same way. This kind of feedback surely warranted further investigation, don't you think? Wouldn't you be curious?

They didn't. They weren't.

(I didn't mention the store manager's name in case he still works there and his boss is reading this. I wouldn't want him to get canned.)

Never make the same mistake as our marketing team. Feedback is vital in any business - and the stuff that rocks your paradigm is usually the most valuable.

TRIZ Bitz

1. Set up a customer feedback link on your Web site and have inputs automatically e-mailed to internal managers
2. Ask 12 folks, half who like you and half who don't, to review your manuscript before it goes to print
3. A toilet uses negative feedback to fill itself up with water when flushed

How can you use feedback to improve your product, process, system, or service?

Hello and Goodbye
from John and Jane Doe

January 28, 2008

John and Jane Doe
4321 Happily Thereafter Ave.
Everytown, USA

To the Companies Who Want Our Money,

Yesterday's selling techniques aren't working so good. Have you noticed?

We're betting that your traffic has been trending downward for the past few months. Are we right? (If we're wrong, keep up the good work. You're doing all the right things.)

But if your traffic has, in fact, been trending downward, here are some things for you to think about:

Today's customer expects easy access to information.
And that information includes the price.

Quit trying to romance everything. Cut the hype. Just say it clean and tight, shoulders back, looking us directly in the eye.

Give us the truth with clarity. Transparency. Openhanded disclosure. Nothing hidden behind your back.

If you tell us about a product or service online and we wonder what it costs and we learn the only way you'll tell us the price is if we give up our contact information, we think:

1. You're charging too much and you know it.
2. You want an opportunity to "overcome our objections" or
3. You're planning to contact us and control the conversation with rigged questions under the pretense that you're "consulting" us for our own good.
4. You want us to give you a credit card number,
5. But what you really need is a clue.

Sorry, we don't mean to be rude.

You seem to be sincere in your confusion about why traffic is down and we're just trying to tell you the truth you need to hear.

Yes, it's partly the economy.

But you've also lost touch with the times.

You've got reasons for not disclosing your prices. We understand that. You don't want to give your competitors "the edge" or something or other. But companies with good prices aren't afraid to share them. In their ads. Over the phone. On their websites. From the housetops.

Or at least that's how it seems to us.

Have a great 2008.

John and Jane Doe

34
Intermediary

An Intermediary is a temporary or nonessential component of a product or system which can be easily removed. The intermediary lens can be applied in one of two ways:

1. Use an intermediary carrier article or intermediary process.
    a. i.e. Carpenter's nail set, used between the hammer and the nail

2. Merge one object temporarily with another (which can be easily removed).
    a. i.e. Use a pot holder to carry hot dishes to the table

A consultant is an intermediary in a business environment. The consultant comes in to the company to evaluate a certain aspect of the business or solve a problem and then leaves.

Chemical processes often use this principle. In some chemical reactions, a specific, otherwise unnecessary substance is included as an intermediary. The new chemical, Chemical C's (a catalyst), sole purpose is to make the main chemicals, A and B, react faster or move the process along further.

In the old days, bootleggers used salt as an intermediary to hide their goods. When the bootleggers got a tip that authorities would be coming on board the ship to look for loot, the smugglers would put salt rocks on top of the 55-gallon drums of alcohol. They'd throw the drums overboard, and the salt rocks would cause the containers to sink.

When the authorities searched the ship, the contraband was gone. After a while, the salt would dissolve and the drums would rise back to the surface. The salt rocks served as an intermediary in the bootlegging process; a temporary step to improve the end result.

Intermediaries are even making their way into the legal system. Mediators are quite popular these days in divorce court. Rather than fighting out battles in the courtroom with expensive lawyers and legal fees, couples hire a mediator to help resolve the issues before the parties actually go before a judge. Mediation is big business in today's divorce-happy society.

Give 'Em a Piece of the Action

Sometimes an intermediary is necessary to make a project happen. When I worked for Parker Hannifin, we built flight hydraulic actuators for almost all of the commercial aircraft in the world. Boeing actually builds the airplanes, and Parker Hannifin was sub-contracted to Boeing to build the actuators. Unfortunately, Japanese Airlines would not give Boeing the contract to build airplanes for them unless at least one company in Japan got a piece of the action.

So, we came up with an insane plan to get around this requirement. We still built the hydraulic actuators at Parker-Hannifin, but we shipped the actuators, with a part tag, to a Japanese company. When the product arrived in Japan, all the company had to do was glue the tag onto the actuator – using a glue kit that we supplied to them. The company marked the product up a percentage to make a profit and then sent the actuator back to Boeing.

We did all the work, and then let the Japanese company do 30 seconds of labor to glue the tag on. This extra, although seemingly unnecessary, intermediary step allowed us to say that a Japanese company was included in the process. As a result, the Japanese airlines then agreed to a purchase contract with Boeing.

Boeing was happy to pay the extra shipping costs and the markup; after all, the extra money was a drop in the bucket in comparison to the profit from the contract.

Funny what you'll do to get the job done, isn't it?

TRIZ Bitz
1. Use a travel agent to book your Australia vacation
2. Hire a tax consultant instead of trying to do it yourself
3. Use "Get Friday," your part-time executive assistant, to proofread your proposal

Can you improve your product or business by adding in an intermediary?

35
Self-Service

The lens of Self-Service is exactly as it sounds. This principle is usually applied as follows:

1. Make an object serve itself by performing helpful auxiliary functions.
   a. i.e. A soda fountain pump that runs on the pressure of the carbon dioxide that is used to "fizz" the drinks; this assures that drinks will not be flat and eliminates the need for sensors

2. Use waste resources, energy, or substances.
   a. i.e. Use food and lawn waste to create compost

In other words, Self-Service implies that either the customer or the product serves itself. For instance, the Google algorithm used to generate search results applies the Self-Service lens. The algorithm is a type of Self-Service because the program is constantly updating itself.

Diapers, Diabetes, and Daddies

Medical supplies are a great example of Self-Service. Consider the home pregnancy test. Couples can find out whether or not they've conceived a child without ever leaving the comfort of their own home.

Diabetic testing products are also Self-Service. Blood sugar monitors, insulin pumps, test strips, and meters work to measure insulin levels in the blood stream so that the patient can adjust their medication or insulin supply to keep their levels normal. This self-serve aspect of the testing supplies allows diabetic individuals to lead a more normal life, without having to make constant visits to their physician.

One new product, a do-it-yourself DNA test, allows parents to establish the paternity of their children. The Identigene, sold by Sorenson Genomics of Salt Lake City, lets users answer paternity questions in the comfort and privacy of their own home. The company expects to sell about 52,000 tests this year.[16]

Fast-food restaurants are another application of this lens. When you visit a McDonald's or Burger King, you are your own waiter. You walk to the counter to place your order, fill up your drink, gather your condiments, and pick up your own food. When you are finished eating, you put away your own trash. Fast-food chains rely on this self-service element to keep their prices low.

Look at the recent advancements made in Self-Service centers at grocery stores and home improvement centers. The self-check lane used to be a huge pain for customers. However, in the last year and a half or so, the reliability of these service stations has greatly improved. Customers like scanning and bagging their purchases themselves, rather than having to rely on a cashier – and as consumers continue to flock to these Self-Service centers, more improvements will follow.

Self-Service has also made its way into the airline industry. Fliers can swipe a credit-card at a self-check-in kiosk and get their boarding pass without ever seeing a human agent.

TRIZ Bitz
1. Visit www.selfserviceworld.com and you'll find thousands of self service ideas you can apply to your business
2. ScanBuy software allows you to take a picture of a product barcode with your cell phone camera and

---

[16] Who's your daddy? Answers at the drugstore. MSNBC. JoNel Allecia. http://www.msnbc. msn.com/id/23814032/. Accessed 27 Mar. 2008.

automatically sends competitor pricing

3. A self-service happy hour in the hotel lobby

Is there an element of your product, service, or business that could be made Self-Service?

36
Copying

The lens of Copying instructs users to use simple, inexpensive copies of their product or service. This lens is usually applied in one of three ways:

1. Instead of an unavailable, expensive, or fragile object, use simpler and inexpensive copies.
   a. i.e. Listen to an audiotape instead of attending a seminar

2. Replace an object or process with optical copies.
   a. i.e. Measure an object by measuring the photograph

3. If visible optical copies are already used, move to infrared or ultraviolet copies.
   a. i.e. Make images in infrared to detect heat sources, such as diseases in crops, or intruders in a security system

Copying can solve many problems in a business. The copy can be a replication of a part, product, service, or even an experience.

Learning to Fly and Fire

Perhaps the most obvious example is a flight simulator. Rather than paying for the rental or purchase of an airplane, a would-be pilot can start learning to fly via a flight simulation. A significant portion of a pilot's instrument flight training can be done on a simulator. The pilot does not have to actually be in the plane to begin learning the basics of how to fly.

The military uses virtual reality in Basic Training to prepare soldiers for combat. Soldiers are desensitized to killing enemies through the use of video games and virtual reality technology. Obviously the Army can't use real people to prepare their soldiers to kill, so they use the next best thing – a copy.

Applications of this lens are abundant in our digital world. For example, consider video conferencing, document scanning and faxing, e-learning programs, and eBooks. Video conferencing allows participants to interact in a meeting without having to physically be in the same location.

Similarly, document scanning or faxing allows for a cheap copy of a document to be quickly and easily sent to multiple destinations around the world. Rather than sending the original via the post office, a user can simply scan in the document and instantly send the paperwork wherever it needs to go.

E-learning programs, or distance learning, allow students to complete technical programs, trade school, or college courses from the comfort of their own home. Students can get a degree without ever having to step foot in a physical classroom. The virtual course is a "copy" of the real thing.

An eBook is essentially identical to a printed book, except that the manuscript is published digitally. eBooks are much cheaper to produce and make it possible for anyone to become a published author. YouTube operates on a similar principle. Rather than making physical copies of a recording, such as a DVD or VHS, the creator can post their masterpiece online for the whole world to see – without ever spending a penny.

TRIZ Bitz

1. Use 3D printing services or stereo lithography to make your first prototype
2. Post all of your user manuals online in a PDF format and make them easy to find
3. Swiffer wet disposable cloths revolutionized mops

How can you Copy your product, service, or system to cut costs or make your product more accessible to consumers in distant locations?

37
Cheap Disposables

Paper plates, disposable razors and cameras, and lighters are all inexpensive products that can be thrown away after one use. Obviously, there's no need to bring expensive china on a camping trip or picnic – and a disposable camera is usually preferred for a trip to the water park over an expensive digital version.

Disposable diapers, plastic cups, and many medical supplies operate on the same principle. These objects are simple, inexpensive copies of the real thing, which serve their purpose and can be thrown away afterward.

This lens is technically defined as, "Replacing an inexpensive object with a multiple of inexpensive objects, compromising certain qualities such as service life, for instance."

In other words, create an inexpensive copy of your product – or an intermediary product – that can be easily replicated and disposed of after use.

Button Up

When I worked on the space shuttle program, I remember struggling to find just the right material to grit-blast some parts on the Solid Rocket Boosters. We needed a material that wasn't too hard, and not too soft. We experimented with many different types of materials because when you're grit-blasting a part, you want to be able to clean the part up and create a pristine surface to bond to. However, you don't want to take away too much metal because the metal cases have to be reused. The metal cases get thinner and thinner from the grit-blasting, and when they get too thin they become fragile and can no longer be used due to the pressure requirements.

Ironically enough, one of the best materials we found was plastic buttons, or rather the pieces ejected from the buttons  to create holes for threading. Those tiny little dots of plastic were inexpensive, and basically a scrap product in button manufacturing – yet they worked really well as a grit-blast media.

TRIZ Bitz
1. BIC disposable lighter made almost all normal lighters obsolete
2. Disposable diaphragm that required no inspection, cleaning, and is not messy
3. Virtual war game where no one really gets killed

Can you improve your product or service using cheap, short-lived disposables?

38
Mechanical Interaction Substitution

Waiting for the FTIR machine to warm up is about as exciting as watching paint dry.

I studied Chemical Engineering in college, and I was assisting Dr. Holland with some research work for the Oak Ridge National Laboratory. We were making a chemical soup for them, a caustic recipe with ingredient names that I forgot years ago.

Oak Ridge said they could tell us what the soup was for, but then they'd have to kill us. Sometimes ignorance is bliss.

The soup was suspended in an aqueous solution, which is scientist lingo for "suspended in water." Part of the research required us to test the concentration of the samples before we sent them off to Oak Ridge.

To test the concentration we used an FTIR machine. FTIR stands for *Fourier Transform Infrared Spectroscopy*. (In case you were wondering, no, the machine did not come with a flux capacitor.)

This beast of a machine was a major drain on my social life; each time we got ready to test a sample's concentration, the machine had to warm up for two hours! To make things worse, the lab procedures stated that we were not allowed to leave the machine unattended while turned on.

I have no idea why that requirement was in place; maybe it was standard-issue student torture, but sitting there for two hours each time seemed ridiculous, especially when you consider the test itself took only five minutes.

The soup was purple. At least that is what I called the color then; now I guess I would say that the color was better described as a shade of fuchsia (this unfortunate knowledge may be due to my nasty exposure to Danielle Steele). Anyway, I had noticed that the intensity of the color changed based on its concentration. I could pretty much guess what the concentration was going to be before I even stuck the sample in the machine.

Then it hit me.

What's the tolerance required on the concentration measurement? I had never read the spec, so I went back to Dr. Holland and asked him. He didn't know either, so I called Oak Ridge.

Oak Ridge informed me that the tolerance was plus or minus five percent. I was furious.

Why the hell was I letting this machine crush my social life if we can live with a range as big as 5%? The FTIR could measure something like 10,000 times more accuracy than that, but that degree of specificity wasn't necessary. The whole situation reminded me of that trap we can all fall into:

Measure with a micrometer, mark with chalk, and cut with an axe

This FTIR was way overkill. I could see plus or minus 5% with my eyes. Easy.

So I made up several different mason jars of different concentrations, labeled them, and put them on the window sill. Then when I got a new sample I simply held the new solution up to the light, compared colors, and guessed at the concentration. I had two to three percent accuracy with just my eyes.

Good enough.

Social life restored. (Not really, I only had one date in the entire four years I was in college, but I figured the story sounded better this way.)

Of course I had never heard of TRIZ or any of the lenses back then, but now I realize that situation was a simple case of mechanical substitution. I exchanged a mechanical machine's results for an optical one – my eye.

The lens of Mechanical Substitution is typically applied in one of four ways:

1. Replace a mechanical means with a sensory (optical, acoustic, taste, or smell) means.
   a. i.e. Replace a physical fence to confine a dog or cat with an acoustic "fence" with a signal audible only to the animal

2. Use electric, magnetic, and electromagnetic fields to interact with the object.
   a. i.e. To mix two powders, electrostatically charge one positive and the other negative. Either use fields to direct them, or mix them mechanically and let their acquired fields cause the grains of powder to pair up.

3. Change from static to movable fields, from unstructured fields to those having structure.
   a. i.e. Early communications used omnidirectal broadcasting. We now use antennas with very detailed structure of the pattern of radiation.

4. Use fields in conjunction with field-activated (such as ferromagnetic) particles.

a. i.e. Heat a substance containing ferromagnetic material by using varying magnetic fields. When the temperature exceeds the Curie point, the material becomes paramagnetic and no longer absorbs heat.

What's that Smell?

Many people don't realize that propane actually has no inherent smell. The foul odor is added intentionally so that people can identify when there is a gas leak in their home. Butane and other hydrocarbons do not have a scent either; the odor is always added. The mechanical means for detecting a leak, such as a mechanical or electrical sensor, are replaced by the sense of smell.

Remote controls are another example of this principle. No one gets off their butts to turn the channel or change the volume anymore. Remotes communicate with their devices via infrared or radio signals. The remote uses electromagnetic fields to interact with the object, rather than forcing the user to physically control the machine.

TRIZ Bitz
1. Black and Decker laser tape measure
2. Use a digital camera to survey property
3. Wireless computer mouse

I was doing more work than necessary in Dr. Holland's lab. Are you making the same mistake? How can you use Mechanical Substitution to replace a mechanical means with a sensory means in your product or service? Could the sense of smell, taste, sound, or sight replace a mechanism in your business?

39
Pneumatics and Hydraulics

Pneumatics and Hydraulics refers to the use of gas and liquid parts of an object instead of solid parts, such as inflatable, liquid-filled, air-cushioned, or hydro-reactive parts. For example, a vehicle can store energy from deceleration in a hydraulic system and then use the stored energy to accelerate later.

Basically, Pneumatics and Hydraulics is the use of a gas or liquid in place of solid parts.

Light as Air

Have you ever seen those really cool, outdoor, inflatable projection screens at conferences or big events? These projection screens are filled with air and can be used to make an instant movie screen. The air-filled screen is greatly preferred to solid, fixed structures that require installation on site. Inflatable projection screens allow users to temporarily transform a location into a high-tech, outdoor movie theater.

I believe air is also the preferable means of travel on a float trip. I frequently go tubing down the river in Utah, and I'm always amazed at how much trouble people have with their kayaks and canoes. Their little boats are constantly getting banged and beaten up by the rocks in the river. My inflatable inner tube, on the other hand, just bounces off obstacles – and there are no issues with rocks. Floating is smooth sailing for me in my air ship.

Air mattresses are another great example of Pneumatics and Hydraulics. Hosts can create an extra bed for their guests by simply pulling the mattress out of the box and inflating the bed. Air beds are much easier to store than an actual mattress, making these pallets a simple solution to providing a comfortable place for guests to rest.

Shoe manufacturers also utilize this principle to make a more comfortable product. As you'll recall from the Universal Network chapter, the Reebok Pump uses an air pump in the shoe soles to give users an extra lift. Dr. Scholl's created shoe sole inserts filled with gel, rather than using an insert filled with a solid material. Are you gelling?

Pneumatics and Hydraulics does not have to be applied literally. For instance, a person can "liquidate" their assets, and convert their funds into cash.

TRIZ Bitz

1. Water knife that can selectively cut pathological tissues without damaging nerves
2. Mars Landers uses airbags to "bounce land" on to the surface
3. Inflatable air travel "U-pillow" converts easily from storage to use

Can you transform a solid part in your business or product into a gas or liquid and improve efficiency?

40
Flexible Shells and Thin Films

"How about Blow-up Dolls?"

After I throw that idea out there, I simply allow the visual to sink in and wait for the expression of disgust, especially from the females in the room.

In the "da Vinci and the 40 Answers workshop," I throw this example out when we get to this lens: *Flexible Shells and Thin Films.* Of course, the audience immediately assumes I am talking about products for romantically-challenged males, but I am not. The example I am talking about is using an inflatable doll, dressed in a cop uniform, as a

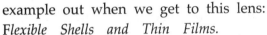

dummy police officer sitting in a parked squad car on the side of the road.

I guarantee you'll hit the brakes as soon as you see this inanimate police man. You can't tell that the doll is not the real thing, until you have already passed by. This sort of illusion is popping up everywhere as a means to get commuters to slow down, without having to pay someone $25 an hour to just sit on their butt holding a radar gun.

Where else would this kind of application work?

The Flexible Shells and Thin Films lens is technically defined as:

1. The use of flexible shells and thin films instead of three-dimensional structures.
   a. i.e. Use inflatable, thin film structures as winter covers on a tennis court or pool

2. Isolating the object from the external environment using flexible shells and thin films.
   a. i.e. Float a film of bipolar material (one end of hydrophilic, one end hydrophobic) on a reservoir to limit evaporation

Consider Tylenol gel capsules. Gel caps get into the consumer's blood stream more quickly than traditional, powder-based tablets, providing faster relief from aches and pains. The thin shell serves to encapsulate the gel in the bottle. The shell dissolves in the digestive tract and the pain reliever is absorbed into the blood stream.

Have you ever noticed that a Coors Light can is a lot thinner than a Budweiser can? The Coors can is made from a very thin piece of aluminum. This thin shell that encases the "Silver Bullet" beer is lightweight and inexpensive to produce. In fact, the aluminum is so thin that the can would not be able to withstand the weight of the cases stacked on top of each other if the can wasn't supported by the pressure of the carbonation in the beer.

Hand warmers and baby bottle warmers are another application of flexible shells and thin films. If you ever examine a hand warmer, you'll see that the warmer is actually encased by a flexible shell. You actually have to remove the packaging and shake or break the contents of the warmer to activate the heating element.

Baby bottle warmers work in much the same way. You boil the warmer to set up a chemical structure inside the bag. Then, you wrap the warmer around the baby bottle. Once you squeeze it, the flexible film inside breaks and allows the warmer to create an exothermic reaction and heat up the bottle.

Protection and Prevention

Two examples that stand out in my mind are surgical gloves and condoms. Surgical gloves have to be strong enough to ensure sanitary conditions for both the patient and the physician. These gloves protect patients from exposure to potentially infectious matter, and guard health professionals from exposure to diseases and viral infections living in bodily fluids.

The condom is designed in a similar fashion. Condoms must be waterproof, elastic, and durable to protect people from sexually transmitted diseases and to prevent unwanted pregnancies. At the same time, this protective layer has to be thin enough so as not to hinder the sensations of sexual intercourse.

A flexible shell or thin film does not have to be a physical object. Many corporations utilize "open door policies" that encourage employees to address their grievances with the company's executives or CEO when the employee believes middle management will be either unable to resolve the conflict or will retaliate against the employee for making the complaint. The open door policy is symbolic of a thin shell because employees can break through the company hierarchy to access upper-level management without hindrance.

TRIZ Bitz

1. Hard contact lenses replaced by "soft"
2. Soccer shin guards for improved flexibility and comfort
3. Bicycle seat made of thin padding over a flexible shell that uniquely shapes to the individual

How could the application of a Flexible Shell or Thin Film improve your product or service?

259

Tomorrow Has Come.

When *The Cluetrain Manifesto* was published in 1999, it smacked of silly futurism, like Maxwell Smart's shoe-phone and Dick Tracey's TV-wristwatch.

Both of which are now possible.

Likewise, the societal shift predicted by *The Cluetrain* is already happening. Can you feel it?

Here's a look at a few of the **95 Theses** of *The Cluetrain Manifesto*. These statements were laughed at when they first appeared 8 years ago, but no one's laughing anymore:

1. Markets are conversations.
Are your ads a conversation with your customer, or are they a pompous lecture?

2. Markets consist of human beings, not demographic sectors.
Are you marketing to people with names and faces and favorite places, or are you marketing to a "target"?

3. Conversations among human beings sound human. They are conducted in a human voice.
Are your ads written the way people talk, or the way ads talk?

4. Whether delivering information, opinions, perspectives, dissenting arguments or humorous asides, the human voice is typically open, natural, uncontrived.
Would the public describe your ads as "open, natural and uncontrived"?

15. In just a few more years, the current homogenized "voice" of business – the sound of mission statements and brochures – will seem as contrived and artificial as the language of the 18th-century French court.
Wow. That's already happening. You've noticed it, haven't you?

22. Getting a sense of humor does not mean putting some jokes on the corporate web site. Rather, it requires big values, a little humility, straight talk, and a genuine point of view.
What are your values? Do you admit your mistakes? Do you talk straight, or go sideways? Are you willing to say what you really think?

23. Companies attempting to "position" themselves need to take a position. Optimally, it should relate to something their market actually cares about.

I've said it often: "Most ads aren't written to persuade. They're written not to offend." Do you have the courage to take a position and suffer the wrath of those who disagree? Will you choose who to lose?

24. Bombastic boasts – "We are positioned to become the preeminent provider of XYZ" – do not constitute a position.

In my 1998 book, **The Wizard of Ads,** *the fourth of my Twelve Most Common Mistakes in Advertising (chapter 35) was:* **"Unsubstantiated Claims.** *Advertisers often claim to have what the customer wants, such as 'highest quality at the lowest price,' but fail to offer any evidence. An unsubstantiated claim is nothing more than a cliché the prospect is tired of hearing. You must prove what you say in every ad. Do your ads give the prospect new information? Do they provide a new perspective? If not, be prepared to be disappointed with the results."*

Is your business in step with the fast-coming future?

Roy H. Williams

41
Porous Materials

According to *American Heritage Dictionary*, porous is defined as "full of or having pores; admitting the passage of gas or liquid through pores or interstices; easily crossed or penetrated." Porous Materials is usually applied as follows.

1. Make an object porous or add porous elements such as inserts or coatings.
   a. i.e. Drill holes in a structure to reduce the weight

2. If an object is already porous, use the pores to introduce a useful substance or function.
   a. i.e. Use a porous metal mesh to wick excess solder away from a joint

Deck design relies heavily on the addition of porous elements. Most people don't think about a deck in this way, but one of the most important things about designing outdoor decks is to make sure the gap between the planks of wood is big enough, or porous enough, to allow water and dirt to flow through. On the other hand, you can't make the gaps so large that a woman's heel would get stuck in the space.

If you've ever been to a wedding reception or other formal event where many of the women are wearing heels, you'll know that poor deck design can be a nightmare. Women step in between the planks and break off their heels, and it's just not a pretty picture. However, the porous gaps are a necessary element of the deck's design to allow for the release of external elements (i.e., dirt and water).

In the Western part of the U.S., many people do not have air conditioning units. Instead, swamp coolers, also known as sump coolers, are used to cool homes and office buildings. Swamp coolers are evaporative coolers. The cooler uses a porous mat that allows water to flow through and evaporate. A fan draws air through the vents on the sides of the machine, which is then run through the porous pads. The heat in the air evaporates the water from the pads, allowing cooled, moist air to be delivered into the building.

"Porous Materials" does not have to be applied literally. Your business can be made porous through the use of customer advisory boards, an open house, or allowing customers to sit in on a meeting. Find ways to let the customers into your business.

The Complaint Sponge

I've always thought that there should be a customer complaint sponge in restaurants and hotels. Imagine if there were a person whose sole responsibility was to be porous and soak up customer complaints like a sponge. Customers love to complain, so why not make listening to their issues a full-time job? Customers would be happier knowing that their voice was being heard, and the rest of the employees would be thrilled that they weren't having to listen.

If a customer was unsatisfied with the degree of customer service, or was unhappy with an aspect of the product, they'd know exactly who to talk to. The customer complaint sponge shouldn't be another guy standing around in the lobby in a sport coat; they should be dressed in a different kind of uniform (maybe like a sponge!), so that everyone would know that person's sole responsibility was to listen to complaints.

TRIZ Bitz

1. A hiking vest which incorporates a porous polyester shell to reflect the sun's rays and to allow air to flow freely through it
2. A porous marine matting that protects your boat, your feet, and your dock
3. Porous pavement with a stone reservoir underneath that temporarily stores surface runoff

How can you make your company or product more porous?

42
Color/Clarity Changes

"Do you remember when Dr. Yarborough gave me a 9 and you a 10 on that pop quiz?"

"No, not really."

"The score was out of a *100*!! "

"Oh…yeah…now I remember."

Mitch Culbreath and I had not spoken since college, which had been some 25 years ago. He had googled my name on a whim, found me, and picked up the phone. After we covered the basics – jobs, where we live, pets, and so on – I asked him what his wife did for a living.

He told me she was a "color consultant."

"A what?"

"Yeah… that's what all the guys say."

Roy Williams' latest project, *Thought Particles*, is based around the intriguing question: "What is the smallest unit of Thought?"

Only after science had deconstructed matter into its constituent components – its smallest particles – were we able to design substances with the specific characteristics we desired.

Similarly, if we want to design an idea, make an accurate statement, transfer a feeling, capture a mood, paint a mental picture, send a signal, or persuade a person, we must craft a message with specific characteristics. We do this by consciously or unconsciously arranging the constituent components of thought: *thought particles.*

That's really all I want to say about thought particles here; that subject matter could fill many volumes of books. I mention thought particles because the results of this research revealed that we communicate through 12 languages of the mind. One of these languages is color.

Knowing this, I am always curious and intrigued if I can learn more from people who are experts in color. Of course I had to have a chat with Mitch's wife.

Mitch's "color consultant" wife's name is Robin Culbreath and she is the founder of Robin Culbreath Limited. Robin is the creator of TrendLab Report: the foremost consumer lifestyle design trend and color forecast report.

"Mark, I hate to say this, but most men just don't get what I do. I think it took Mitch nine months before he finally understood. What I do is this; I identify, interpret, and translate consumer lifestyle design trends and color for primarily the home furnishings industry, but others as well."

As I spent more and more time with Robin, I finally started to understand what she does. She does infinitely more than just "consult on color." But for our purposes, let's stick to the color discussion because it is extremely powerful.

Robin looks at trends and predicts what product manufacturers should be making a few years in the future, including what colors are going to be hot. Trends can last three to seven years and one of the primary things manufacturers can do over these years, to keep the product looking fresh and to give it longevity, is to change its color and manage the color evolution over time.

Making color changes to a product is infinitely cheaper than changing the actual design and retooling the product.

You can dramatically extend the life of a product line by changing the product's color and keeping the look fresh.

Here is a great example that Robin shared with me. 3M Post-it Notes have had the same line of neon colors for years. Robin spent months and months convincing 3M that the Post-it Notes were in dire need of a color face-lift. Not everyone likes neon, you know.

She was finally successful in getting her "Sweet Pea" selection of colors approved, but she almost didn't get one radical new color approved as part of the package. It took many, many meetings to get that final color approved and added into the color selection. Robin had to go all the way to the top of the 3M food chain for approval.

What was this radical new color, you ask?

White.

In her industry they have a popular phrase;

> Color sells, but the **right** color sells better.

The principle of Color/Clarity Changes is usually applied in one of two ways:

1. Change the color of an object or its external environment.
   a. i.e. Use safe lights in a photographic darkroom.
2. Change the transparency of an object or its external environment.

a. i.e. Use photolithography to change transparent material to a solid mask for semiconductor processing. Similarly, change mask material from transparent to opaque for silk-screen processing.

In other words, Color/Clarity Change refers to a change in color or transparency.

Clarity and Transparency

Have you ever seen the eyeglasses that change in tint? The tint of the glasses becomes darker when worn outside, to the point that the regular glasses can serve as sunglasses. When you walk back inside, the sunglasses' transparency increases, and the lenses become clear again. The tint, or transparency, of the glasses adjusts according to the level of lighting in the environment.

Toy manufacturers also utilize transparency when packaging their products. Have you ever had to open a product while standing in the aisle of a department store so that you can see and touch the product inside? Toy manufacturers eventually got smart and designed their packaging so that kids and parents can actually see the toy within the box.

Clarity also plays a role in sports. NASCAR and Motocross drivers use tear away visors to improve their vision clarity on the road. Rather than wiping away the mud and dust from their visors, they just tear away the top layer to create greater clarity.

Clarity does not apply strictly to tangible objects. The Tylenol scare in the early 1980s (which we discussed earlier in this book), is a great example of clarity change from a non-technical View Point. After seven consumers died as a result of ingesting potassium-cyanide laced capsules, Tylenol's management was very transparent and took full responsibility for their actions. Tylenol executives promised to take prompt action to prevent a similar situation from ever occurring again.

Even though the capsules were believed to have been tampered with by an outside source, Tylenol stepped up to the plate and took full responsibility for the deaths. Their transparency and willingness to accept fault for the situation made the fallout far less severe than it could have been.

How did Iomega become a billion dollar company in the 90s with the Zip Drive? They took existing technology and substituted the boring off-white colored plastic exterior that every other company used with **Cobalt Blue.**

TRIZ Bitz
1. Plant "sticks" that change color 2 days before they need water
2. Fiat car design that changes color based on the environment
3. Mood rings change color based on how you feel

Color and clarity can make a world of difference in your product or business profit and productivity. Can you look through the lens of color and clarity to find a solution for your problem or to improve your product or service? Can you give your product a face-lift with color?

Clarity is the New Creativity

In the language of academics:
The central executive of working memory is the new battleground for marketers. Writers are successfully surprising Broca, thereby gaining the momentary attention of the public, but an absence of salience remains.

In the language of newscasters:
Are your ads gaining the attention of the public but failing to get results? Find out why and learn exactly what you can do about it. Stay tuned for complete details. (Insert commercial break here.)

In the language of the street:
Ads have gotten more creative, but they haven't gotten more convincing. This sucks for advertisers and the public isn't helped by it, either.

In the language of clarity:
Can your product be differentiated?
Can you point out that difference quickly?
Can you explain why the difference matters?
This is effective marketing.

To differentiate your product powerfully and clearly:
1. See it through the eyes of the public.
       (Insiders have too much knowledge.)
2. Ignore everything that doesn't matter.
3. Focus on what the public actually cares about.
4. Say it in the fewest possible words.
5. Close the loopholes by anticipating the
    customer's unspoken questions.

Roy H. Williams

43
Homogeneity

Homogeneity refers to:

1. Making objects interact with a given object of the same material, or material with identical properties.
   a. i.e. Make a diamond-cutting tool out of diamonds

Cut from the Same Mold

Containers and packaging are often made from the same material as the contents to reduce chemical reactions and product waste.

For instance, if you've ever worked with polystyrene chips, you might have noticed that the bag is usually made from the same material as the chips. You don't have to pour the bag's contents into the mixer; instead, you can just throw the whole bag in intact.

Another example is the use of cotton thread to sew cotton material. The cotton fibers in the thread and the material are identical, and as such can be treated and cared for in the same manner.

Natural light bulbs operate on a similar principle. These bulbs create a close replication of sunlight in an indoor room. The light outdoors is homogeneous with the light indoors, creating a more natural environment. The light bulbs are so effective and so similar to natural sunlight, that they're often used to treat Seasonal Affective Disorder (SAD), and help individuals with sight problems.

In a way, ice cream cones are another example of this lens. The ice cream cone holds the ice cream, and you eat both parts. The cone, or holder, is a homogeneous mixture; the holder doesn't exist alone, rather it gets eaten with the contents and is part of the process.

Alternatively, think of a movie sequel. The sequel is created from the same material as the original. The characters, setting, and premise remain homogenous; in many cases, the sequel is simply an extension of the original film.

TRIZ Bitz

1. Artificial bone material is made with the same properties to strengthen dental implants
2. Plastic bottles can be made from corn so they are biodegradable
3. Make clothes, handbags, shoes, and accessories out of the same material to reduce costs

Can you make your product or service more homogenous, and use identical material or material with identical properties?

44
Discarding and Recovering

Discarding and Recovering is usually applied as follows:

1. Making portions of an object that have fulfilled their functions go away (discard by dissolving or evaporating) or modify these directly during operation.
    a. i.e. Use a dissolving capsule for medicine

2. Conversely, restore consumable parts of an object directly in operation.
    a. i.e. Self-sharpening lawn mower blades

In other words, Discarding and Recovering aims to make things go away after their use has been fulfilled, or repairs itself so that the part does not need to be replaced.

Medical practitioners utilize this principle daily. Consider dissolvable stitches, also known as absorbable sutures, and screws that dissolve in surgery. Absorbable sutures are made of materials that break down in body tissue after a known period of time. The disappearing aspect of the stitches is an advantage, especially when the stitches are used internally, because there are no foreign objects left in the patient's body. There's also no need for follow-up appointments to remove the stitches or screws because the apparatus discards itself.

Temporary tattoos are another example. The body art serves a temporary purpose, and then disappears after a few days. Breath strips work in a similar manner. The breath strips serve a temporary purpose, to alleviate bad breath, and then dissolve in your mouth.

Dry ice blasting is a popular process for preparing or cleaning a surface. Dry ice blasting is similar to sand, plastic, bead, or soda blasting, but with one distinct advantage. This process utilizes dry ice particles, which are made from carbon dioxide. When the dry ice particles fall on the ground, they disappear because dry ice sublimes at room temperature. As a result, there's no residue or mess to clean up, because all of the blast material has disappeared.

TRIZ Bitz

1. Crock-Pot liners that you throw away after one use
2. Creams that make stretch marks go away after pregnancy
3. Drano disappears after it has removed the clog

Can you make an unnecessary aspect of your product or services disappear after its use has been fulfilled?

45
Parameter Changes

The principle of Parameter Change is usually applied in one of four ways:

1. Change an object's physical state to a gas, liquid, or solid.
   a. i.e. Freeze the liquid centers of candies and then dip the centers in melted chocolate, rather than handling the messy, gooey, hot liquid

2. Change the concentration or consistency.
   a. i.e. Liquid soap is more concentrated than bar soap, which makes it easier to dispense in the correct amount, and is more sanitary when shared by more than one person

3. Change the degree of flexibility
   a. i.e. Vulcanize rubber to change its flexibility and durability

4. Change the temperature.
   a. i.e. Lower the temperature of medical specimens to preserve them for later analysis

Melts in your Mouth, Not in Your Hands

Once again, the medical community provides a great example of the application of this lens. Medical plaster, used to make casts, begins with a soft material. The soft material can be wrapped around the affected area, and when it cures, the plaster turns hard.

M&Ms also utilize this principle. M&M's "melt in your mouth, not in your hands." The parameter change was to put a candied coating around the chocolate so the candies don't melt until you put them in your mouth.

Parameter change also refers to flexibility. With gas prices at all-time highs and continuing to rise, many people are finding ways to work from home. Working from home is an example of a parameter change in your job.

Temperature change is also a variation in parameter. For example, you raise the temperature of food in the cooking process. Cooking at a higher temperature changes the taste, aroma, textures, and chemical properties of the food.

TRIZ Bitz
1. Floating candles in colored oil
2. Concentrated energy drinks
3. Powdered milk allows longer storage and more efficient transportation

How can you change the parameters of your product or service to improve the physical state, concentration, consistency, or flexibility of your product?

46
Phase Transitions

A Phase Transition uses phenomena occurring during phase transitions, such as volume changes and the loss or absorption of heat. For example, unlike most other liquids, water expands when frozen.

Hannibal and Hot Air Balloons

Hannibal is reputed to have used this principle when marching on Rome. There were large rocks blocking his passage through the Alps. Hannibal supposedly poured water in the cracks of the rocks at night. The cold night air froze the water, and the expansion to a solid state split the rocks into small pieces that could be easily pushed aside.

Think about the way refrigerators and condensers work. These machines use the phase transition of gas to a liquid. As high-pressure, superheated vapor travels through the condenser, the vapor loses heat and undergoes a phase transition to become a cooled liquid. The heat can then be extracted and used to heat a home. In a refrigerator, the heat is taken from inside the fridge and released into the environment. Have you ever felt the warm air on your feet while standing in front of the refrigerator? The heat is the by-product of the phase transition.

One of the biggest selling points of Guinness beer is the creaminess of the drink. The creamy texture is achieved by injecting nitrogen into the beer. The nitrogen changes the phase of the beer, making it a more gaseous and creamy solution. The phase transition of the beer gives it unique properties not found in other ales.

Did you know that hot air balloons run on propane? Most

277

people think of propane as the gas or vapor stored in their barbecue grill tank. However, the average hot air balloon is approximately 90,000 cubic feet and requires a lot of pounds per second of fuel. A standard propane tank doesn't work because you have to burn a lot of propane quickly to be able to generate enough energy to heat the entire balloon.

You can't burn vapor and have enough energy per second, and you can't run vapor from the tank to the burner because you can't move enough pounds per second. So, hot air balloons use propane tanks that differ from your traditional barbecue grill tanks. These tanks allow *liquid* propane to come out of the tanks, up to the burner, and run coils around the flame in such a way that liquid is moved in a much stronger and larger mass up to the burner. The propane changes from a liquid to a vapor at the flame point.

The only way to get enough pounds per second of energy to the burner is to have a phase transition and turn the propane from a liquid to a gas immediately before it is burned. Hot air balloons require that the propane undergo this phase transition.

TRIZ Bitz

1. Web designers transition to volunteers to create "Katrinalist," a web platform to reunite lost families
2. Software companies that transition into a new phase of open source code
3. Use of Vitamin E to reduce hot flashes during menopause

> Would a phase transition make your product
> or service more efficient or profitable?

2008: Year of Transition

In January of 2004 I launched a public presentation: **Society's 40-year Pendulum.** Audiences from Stockholm to Sydney to Vancouver to Myrtle Beach will recall my statement, "2003 was the first year in a 6-year transition from the Idealist perspective to the Civic."

2008 will be the sixth and final year of that transition.

Labels like Baby Boomer and Gen-X and Soccer Mom assume a person's outlook is determined by when they were born. This is a very foolish assumption.

Look around and you'll see that Baby Boomers aren't Boomers anymore. Most have adopted an entirely new outlook and are becoming part of what's happening now. By the end of 2008 there won't be a Baby Boomer left in America. The last, reluctant holdout will finally admit that Woodstock is over, Kennedy is dead, and the Idealism of the 60s was a wistful dream.

In their 1993 book, *Generations,* Strauss and Howe asserted that western society swings from an Idealist outlook to a Civic perspective and back again with the precision of pendulum. And at the bottom of each arc, the new views introduced by that generation's youth will be adopted by the adults within 6 years of the tipping point.

1963 introduced the Idealist outlook we associate with "Baby Boomers." 1968 was the final year of that transition. By 1969, everyone in America, regardless of their age, was seeing through rose-colored lenses.

2003 was 1963 all over again, but this time we're headed in the opposite direction.

2008 will be the last year of our transition to a Civic perspective.

Here's what to remember when selling in 2008:

1. Efficiency is the new Service.
Your customer is saying, "Quality and price and quick, please. I've got things to do. Thanks." Service and selection still matter, but not nearly so much as they once did. Inefficient organizations built on high-touch "relationship" selling will decline. Today's customer is magnetically drawn to efficiency. This attraction will increase over the next few years.

2. Authenticity is essential.
Listen to the street. "Being cool" has become "Keepin' it real."

Naiveté is rare today. Your customer is equipped with a bullshit detector that is highly sensitive and amazingly accurate. And the younger the customer, the more accurate their bullshit detector.

When selling, remember: If you don't admit the downside, they won't believe the upside.

Pulitzer Prize-winning journalist Leonard Pitts gave us an example of "keepin' it real" when he opened his syndicated column recently with the following lines:

I've got nothing against fame. I'm famous myself. Sort of.

OK, not Will Smith famous, or Ellen DeGeneres famous. All right, not even Marilu Henner famous.

I'm the kind of famous where you fly into some town to give a speech before that shrinking subset of Americans who still read newspapers and, for that hour, they treat you like a rock star, applauding, crowding around, asking for autographs.

Then it's over. You walk through the airport the next day and no one gives a second glance. You are nobody again.

Dave Barry told me this story about Mark Russell, the political satirist. It seems Russell gave this performance where he packed the hall, got a standing O. He was The Man. Later, at the hotel, The Man gets hungry, but the only place to eat is a McDonald's across the road. The front door is locked, but the drive-through is still open. So he stands in it. A car pulls in behind him. The driver honks and yells, "Great show, Mark!"

For the record, I consider Leonard Pitts to be one of the greatest living writers in the world today. **Read his column** and see if you don't agree.

3. A Horizontal Connectedness is replacing yesterday's vertical, social hierarchy. Labels like "white collar" and "blue collar" sound almost racist today. The new American dream isn't about pulling ahead and leaving the others behind. It's about becoming a productive member of the team.

"Winning" has become less important than "belonging."

Listen to the streets. "I'm number one," gets the response, "You ain't all that, dog. You ain't all that."

Labor unions were deader than a bag of hammers in 2004, a relic of the past, so when I predicted that collective bargaining would reawaken and gain momentum during the coming Civic outlook, audiences often laughed or folded their arms and curled a lip, thinking I was advocating organized labor. (I wasn't.)

Have you heard about the Hollywood writer's strike? Expect to see Wal-Mart unionized in the upcoming years. Hide and watch. See if I'm not right.

4. Word-of-Mouth is the new Mass Media. Video games and cable TV stripped our kids of their innocence at an early age, but the Technology that robbed them of idyllic childhood also empowered them with cell phones, blogs and blackberries.

Viral marketing wasn't created by the advertising community. It's simply the result of a horizontally-connected generation (1.) sharing their happy discoveries with each other and (2.) trying to protect one another from mistakes.

WHAT THIS MEANS TO BUSINESS: It's no longer enough just to have great advertising. When your customers carry cell phones and can e-mail all their friends with a single click, you need to be exceptionally good at what you do.

5. Boasting is a waste of time.
Your customer is saying, "Talk is cheap. Actions speak louder than words. Don't tell me what you believe. Show me."

IN YOUR ADS, do you include "proofs of claim" your reader, listener or viewer can experience for themselves?

6. Everyone is broken a little.
And the most broken are those who pretend they are not.

It's time to take the advice of Bill Bernbach, "I've got a great gimmick. Let's tell the truth."

7. Keep in mind that during the next 12 months, as we complete the transition from the Idealist outlook to the Civic perspective, these trends will be accelerated by the facts that:
(1.) Access to information is going up and
(2.) Access to money is going down.

By the way, if I ever win a Pulitzer, I'll immediately start wearing French shirts with 3-inch cuff links that spell out PULITZER PRIZE WINNER in diamonds.

But if what I said earlier about "the last, reluctant holdout" is true, I expect my attitude will change approximately one second before midnight on December 31, 2008.

Have a great week.

Roy H. Williams

47
Thermal Expansion

Thermal expansion is usually defined as:

1. The use of thermal expansion, or contraction, of materials.
    a. i.e. Fit a tight joint together by cooling the inner part to contract, heating the outer part to expand, putting the joint together, and returning to equilibrium.

2. If thermal expansion is being used, use multiple materials with different coefficients of thermal expansion.
    a. i.e. The basic leaf-spring thermostat uses two metals with different coefficients of expansion. The metals are links so that it bends one way when warmer than normal and the opposite way when cooler.

An easy way to explain thermal expansion is to consider the problem of a tight jar lid. If you can't undo a lid, you can always heat up the jar to loosen the lid. Similarly, many people use torches to loosen up tight bolts.

My airplane engine is another great example of Thermal Expansion. One of the biggest problems with Cessna aircraft-type engines, also known as combustion engines, is you can shock cool them. If you cut the power and descend too quickly, the engine is cooling very quickly outside while the piston inside is still hot. You end up shrinking the engine around the piston, and you can actually make the engine fail. Pilots have to be very careful upon descent in a piston airplane to avoid engine failure.

The engine in my plane actually uses a combination of water-cooled and air-cooled heads. Because water takes so much longer to undergo a drastic temperature change, you can't shock cool the engine.

A less literal application of Thermal Expansion is mixing up team members in group projects. Pairing someone who is "hot" in their career, with someone who's not, will encourage creativity and productivity in the less outstanding employee.

TRIZ Bitz
1. Relax in a hot tub to cool your temper
2. Use hotter water if material still won't come clean
3. Combine two dissimilar personalities on the project team to balance heated discussions

How could you look through the lens of Thermal Expansion to improve your product or service?

48
Strong Oxidants

The principle of Strong Oxidants is usually applied as follows:

1. Replace common air with oxygen-enriched air.
   a. i.e. Scuba diving with Nitrox or other non-air mixtures for extended endurance

2. Replace enriched air with pure oxygen.
   a. i.e. Cut at a higher temperature using an oxy-acetylene torch

3. Use ionized oxygen.
   a. i.e. Ionize air to trap pollutants in an air cleaner

4. Replace ozonized or ionized oxygen with ozone.
   a. i.e. Speed up chemical reactions by ionizing the gas before use

Strong Oxidants essentially relates to increasing or decreasing the concentration of oxygen in an environment. This lens can be applied especially liberally, and does not necessarily have to relate to the element of oxygen.

Spark Your Creativity

Instead, consider oxygen as an initiative or spark that changes the environment.

A student in my class once asked if I was a gamer or if I knew anything about game-theory training and the ways gamers design games. Although I know almost nothing about the topic, his theory was fascinating because there's a great deal of similarity between game design and Strong Oxidants. The programmer has to make the game interesting to keep players interested in playing to the next level. They also have to make the game challenging enough to keep the player's attention; however, the game can't be too challenging or players will give up and stop playing. There has to be an oxidizing "spark" that keeps players intrigued or else the game will fail.

Guest speakers, seminars, and conferences can also be a strong oxidant. Sending employees off to a convention can spark creativity and drastically change the work environment.

The jester from ancient times is also an example of a Strong Oxidant. The jester's primary role was that of a comedian, but the jester was also a war consultant to the king. In fact, the jester was the only person who was allowed to argue with the generals in front of the king. The generals could come up with a big master plan of how to attack the enemy, only for the jester to laugh and say, "Let's just not show up for a few months and let the soldiers starve to death." (By the way, that plan has actually been used to great success several times throughout history.) The jester was an oxidant because he was allowed to come in and mix things up and tell people that their plan was crazy.

TRIZ Bitz
1. Volunteer to be a big brother or big sister
2. Strong oxidant for your physical and mental health: get a dog
3. Oxygen in a can as a unique gift or party favor

How can you spark creativity and innovation in your business?

The Monster Under My Bed

I learned last week why I'm no good at making small talk. The realization blew my mind.

Pennie and I were sitting in the sun room looking at our computers when she asked, "Did you get the e-mail from Janet?"

"Yes."

"Should I answer it or will you?"

"You, please. I have no idea how to respond."

Pennie smiled her knowing smile and began to type for both of us. Our friend Janet had sent us an e-mail "just to stay in touch." I enjoyed reading it, was glad she had sent it, but when it came to typing a response I was paralyzed.

"How's this?" Pennie asked.

I looked at what she had written and was flabbergasted, "Princess, you are the smartest person in the world."

Pennie smiled, then looked curiously concerned. Closing her computer, she asked, "Why is it so hard for you to make small talk?"

She knows that chitchatting with people is hell for me. Friends who know us casually think of me as quiet and mousy, "the guy who never says anything," or ferociously unfriendly, "the guy with the giant ego."

I looked at Pennie's face and saw she expected an answer.

"Well," I began slowly, "when a person says something like, 'How about this day we're having!' or asks one of those filler questions like, 'How have you been?' every response that pops into my head strikes me as being utterly irrelevant or makes me look completely self absorbed."

That was the Eureka moment. I think I may have actually gasped a little. With giant eyes I whispered, *"It's from all the years of ad writing!"*

People who've seen me speak from a platform know I'm the king of forceful statements, persuasive arguments and ribald ripostes. But social situations require low-impact statements, the kind I guard against every day. I'm the bounty hunter who looks for words without impact and makes them disappear. My job is to keep my clients from

286

making irrelevant statements in their advertising and make sure they never seem self-absorbed.

I'm less embarrassed by my awkwardness now. I think of it almost like a war wound, "Gather 'round, children, and I'll tell you how I got these scars." How's that for putting a spin on it?

Somewhere in this world is the most extraordinary ad writer on earth. I have no idea who he is.

The only thing I can tell you for sure is that he is socially very awkward.

Roy H. Williams

49
Inert Atmosphere

The principle of Inert Atmosphere is typically applied as follows:

1. Replace a normal environment with an inert one.
   a. i.e. Prevent degradation of a hot metal filament by using an argon atmosphere

2. Add neutral parts, or inert additives to an object.
   a. i.e. Increase the volume of powdered detergent by adding inert ingredients. This makes the detergent easier to measure with conventional tools.

We were once moving 300,000-pound rocket segments around a brand new building at the Kennedy Space Center. When the segments come from Utah, there are dozens of accessories that have to be added to them before they are ready to fly. Of course, being a new building, the cranes and structure had not been checked out yet. We didn't want to be testing the reliability of the new building with 300,000-pound pieces of dynamite, so we replaced the Ammonium Perchlorate in the fuel recipe with potassium chloride, an inert substance. The potassium chloride still made the fuel look and feel like a real propellant, but it couldn't burn. Because the substance was inert, we were able to perform many safety operation checks on the facility.

A fire extinguisher is another example of Inert Atmosphere. A Halon fire suppression system works because it takes the three components of fire: fuel, spark, and oxygen, and chemically reacts with them to make them inert.

Can you make a hostile environment more "inert" by eliminating the troublemaker? You can do so by approaching them ahead of time and making the situation more inert for the rest of the team so you can actually get something done. Handle them separately.

TRIZ Bitz

1. Speed dating where the stress of introduction has been eliminated
2. Add inert glass micro balloons to resin to turn it into a paste
3. Quarantine smokers in an airport

What is the cheapest and easiest way to improve a boring or inert room, office space, or building? Paint the walls.

How can you apply the inert concept to you business?

Will You Embarrass Yourself?

Are you anxious to look foolish in front of others?

Will you happily submit yourself to ridicule?

Are you willing to do a thing badly until you've learned to do it well?

Probably not, unless you're the one in five hundred who has what it takes to succeed.

"Only those who dare to fail greatly can ever achieve greatly." – Robert F. Kennedy

The lone pioneer plunges ahead and discovers a world while four hundred and ninety-nine settlers whine for maps and roads.

America was founded by pioneers.

How might we dull a glistening nation?

1. **Pay** the dullest and least impressive to educate the children.
2. **Create** a system of teaching that judges everything as "correct" or "incorrect." This will allow the dull and unimpressive to easily grade the children's tests.
3. **Discourage** exploration.
4. **Reward** conformity. Teach that inside the box is good.
5. **Celebrate** sports. Make sure the children understand that taller, stronger kids have natural advantages that cannot be overcome. Build stadiums and hire announcers to shout the names of students who display physical dominance.
6. **Minimize** school concerts and science fairs and art shows. Treat them as though they're for losers. Have them in the school cafeteria.

Follow these 6 Simple Steps and you can expect:

1. **Drop-Outs.** Currently, 38 percent of America's children are dropping out of high school and that number is rising.
2. **Cloned Repetition**. Have you noticed that every mall has exactly the same stores as every other mall and that every city has all the same restaurants?
3. **Death of Industry**. The cars of once-mighty GM and Ford no longer excite us. We want cars designed by the children of foreigners.
4. **Street Gangs.** If school taught us anything, it's that physical dominance is the key to reward.

An outsider, observing how we educate our children, would be forced to conclude that we value:
1. Efficient mediocrity, and
2. Going in circles

But do we really want to become a nation of Wal-Mart shoppers and NASCAR fans?

Jeffrey Eisenberg told me that last line would horribly offend you. I hope he was wrong.

Princess Pennie said that bright, motivated school teachers would feel marginalized and attacked. This certainly wasn't my intention. I know that every school has two or three dazzling teachers who are committed to doing all they can within the current, flawed system. These teachers know they could earn twice the money in the private sector but they're selling their lives just as surely as any other missionary, and they deserve our respect and admiration. But such teachers are the exception, not the rule.

America's school system needs a major overhaul. My goal today is to remind you that, "If we don't change direction soon, we're likely to arrive where we are headed."

Unleash the hounds.

Roy H. Williams

50
Composite Materials

The final lens, Composite Materials, is defined as changing from uniform to composite materials. For instance, composite epoxy resin/carbon fiber golf club shafts are lighter, stronger, and more flexible than metal shafts.

- Reinforced concrete
- Honeycomb structures
- Airplanes and composites
- A cardboard box
- Wood – the world's best *overall* composite

Have you heard of the Space Elevator project for placing satellites in orbit without the need for rockets?

The space elevator "concept" has been around for a long time, but has never been practical until now.

The analogy is this; take a ball and string. If you tie the string to the ball and swing the ball around, the string will get tight and the ball remains at a fixed distance from your hand due to centrifugal force.

The earth is spinning around at a thousand miles an hour. If you had a really long string (50,000 miles) and a ball at the end of it and tied it to the ground, the same centrifugal force of the earth spinning around at a speed of 1,000 miles per hour would do the same thing; hold the string tight, straight upward toward space!

Then satellites could crawl up the string and let go of themselves in orbit.

The problem is there's never been a "string" material that is light enough and strong enough to not fall back to earth due to gravity – until now.

We have come full circle back to Buckminster Fuller. Throughout the history of modern science, carbon has only come in 2 forms: graphite and diamond. Now there is a third. This form is not new, it has always existed in nature but science has just missed it until now.

Bucky Balls were discovered in 1985 by Robert Curl, Harold Kroto, and Richard Smalley at the University of Sussex and Rice University, and are named after Richard Buckminster Fuller.

Because this "new" form of carbon astonishingly resembles Buck's geodesic dome, the scientists have named the discovery Bucky Balls.

Bucky Balls are the lightest and strongest material man has ever known. The material is so strong and so light, the Space Elevator concept can become a reality, along with a billion other new products.

Just Google Space Elevator; you'll be amazed.

TRIZ Bitz

1. Use Photoshop to combine several images into a composite
2. Stack multiple solar panels of different absorbance frequencies to create a more efficient composite design
3. GasBuddy is a Google composite mash up of Google maps and the lowest pump prices

Conclusion

Lenny, Hank, Buck, and Walt were revolutionaries of their time who changed the shape, scope, and direction of the world we live in today. Many of these great men were not recognized for their incredible accomplishments or the significance of their achievements during their own lifetimes; in fact, most of these men were perceived by their peers as misfits and rejects who didn't have a clear grasp on reality. Perhaps Sigmund Freud explained society's underestimation of their genius best in his description of Lenny as "a man who awoke too early in the darkness while the others were still asleep."

Lenny, Hank, Buck, and Walt did not describe their methods for creativity and innovation as "The Basics." Although these innovators could not have been conscious of their common link, I believe their thought processes are evidence of their mutual greatness. Like many of the great thinkers of our time, their creativity flew from them unconsciously, leaving them blissfully unaware of the uniqueness of their thoughts.

We've uncovered the "basics" of these four men's creative thought processes and examined how these principles align with the "tactics" of TRIZ. As these great thinkers have proved, creativity and innovation *can* be taught.

The Basics: Peel the Onion, Try It, Sensible Design, Clear as Mud, View Point, Universal Network, and Ideal Final Result, as well as The Tactics, the 40 Universal Answers of TRIZ, are **deliberate messages and deliberate tools to generate ideas quickly and spark creativity and innovation.**

I strive to give my readers and students this tool set so they can consciously harness the incredible power that drove Lenny,

Hank, Buck, and Walt's creative genius and come up with some crazy, wonderful, new ideas of their own.

At the Wizard Academy, we celebrate the weirdos, renegades, and mavericks of the world. We celebrate the wisdom of absurdity and audacity and understand the importance of thinking outside the box. We encourage people to escape into their right brain and strive to teach these right-brain concepts in a way that everyone can comprehend.

It is my greatest hope that you use the tools of the Basics and the Tactics to one day change your own world. I hope that you share your newfound knowledge and help others escape from the cage of their left brain and the restrictiveness of what "can't be done."

I hope that you can walk away from this book with some truly great and unique ideas that will change the way you do business – and the way that you approach life.

Afterward

Remember James Michener's advice to his students to take ceramics and eurhythmic dancing? How many got off their butts and actually did it? Are you going to put this book away and say, "Yeah, I get it," but then not do a single thing differently?

I sure hope not.

You have to take what you learned and apply the knowledge to your business and life. This book won't do you a bit of good if you just fall back into "the-way-we've-always-done-it mode."

So go out there and apply the tools and concepts I have talked about – and when you do, I want to hear about your experience.

Free Marketing and PR for your Company

My next book, currently in the works, is called *da Vinci and 40 Answers, Success Stories*. I am collecting stories from readers who took the initiative, applied some of the lessons in this book, and made a difference.

Send me your story and you'll get some really great marketing and PR for your company *for free*. Your company and story may be showcased in:

- The book – *da Vinci and the 40 Answers, Success Stories*
- My corporate workshops
- My keynote presentations

Submitting your success story is a great way to get some additional exposure for your company in the most positive light imaginable. You will be showcased as a leading-edge thinker and doer in your industry. You'll be recognized as a leader in creativity and innovation.

So go ahead and just send me a short description of your story. Or, if you want to just contact me to say hello, visit the da Vinci and the 40 answers Web site at:

www.davinciandthe40answers.com

Let's roll!

Glossary

40 Universal Answers – also known as the 40 Principles of TRIZ; the answers to the 1,500 basic problems.

Brainstorming Rules – a list of 10 rules that should be utilized in brainstorming sessions to achieve the optimal result.

Broca's Area – the part of the brain that serves as the gatekeeper for keeping boring experiences out of your memory. Broca's area only allows unusual, exciting, or otherwise unexpected things to be stored in your brain.

Buckminster Fuller – (July 12, 1895 to July 1, 1983) best known for the creation of the geodesic dome, Fuller was a philosopher who once embarked on "an experiment to discover what the little, penniless, unknown individual might be able to do effectively on behalf of all humanity."

Duality – the concept of equal but opposite; a dual state or quality, composed or consisting of twofold or double character or nature

Genrikh Altshuller – (October 15, 1926 to September 24, 1998) a Russian engineer, scientist, journalist, and writer; famed for his creation of TRIZ, a model-based technology for generating innovative ideas and solutions.

Ideal Final Result – Describes the solution to a problem, without jargon, independent of the mechanism or constraints of the original problem; the ultimate idealistic solution of a problem when the desired result is achieved by itself.

Left Brain – the hemisphere of the brain that uses analytical thought; uses vertical, rational, deductive, and sequential logic. The left brain is the predominant mode of thought for most individuals.

Leonardo da Vinci – (April 15, 1452 to May 2, 1519) a polymath: architect, anatomist, sculptor, engineer, inventor, geometer, futurist, and painter; Leonardo conceived visions of technology and innovation that were vastly ahead of his time.

Right Brain – the hemisphere of the brain that uses pattern recognition and horizontal thought; uses systemic logic to solve not only one specific problem, but all other problems that are connected to the issue. The right brain is tied to intuition.

SBIR – Small Business Innovation Research; a government grant program designed to encourage collaboration between the public and private sectors and stimulate technological innovation opportunities for small business owners.

Scientific Method – a problem-solving process; attempts to prove a theory by demonstrating that the theory cannot be disproved.

The Basics – the principles of thought used as the foundation for establishing a creative mindset. The basics are: Peel the Onion, Try It, Sensible Design, Clear as Mud, View Point, Universal Network, and Ideal Final Result.

The Tactics – real-life solutions to universal problems, based on the 40 Universal Answers or Principles of TRIZ.

TRIZ – (pronounced trees) created by Genrikh Altshuller, TRIZ is the Russian acronym for The Theory of Inventing Problem Solving, a model-based technology for generating innovative ideas and solutions. Originally designed to solve engineering and design issues, however, the principles of TRIZ are now being successfully applied to both social issues and business dilemmas.

Walt Disney – (December 5, 1901 to December 15, 1966) one of the most influential and innovative figures in the 20th century entertainment industry; famed for his creativity and ability to communicate the "big picture."

Wizard Academy – a 21st Century Business School; founded in 2000.

Words of the Wizard – insights from Wizard Academy founder and one of the top business thinkers of today, Roy H. Williams. Roy's Memo can also be found at www.mondaymorningmemo. com.

Index

What is Wizard Academy?

Composed of a fascinating series of workshops led by some of the most accomplished instructors in America, Wizard Academy is a progressive new kind of business and communications school whose stated objective is to improve the creative thinking and communication skills of sales professionals, internet professionals, business owners, educators, ad writers, ministers, authors, inventors, journalists and CEOs.

Founded in 1999, the Academy has exploded into a worldwide phenomenon with an impressive fraternity of alumni who are rapidly forming an important worldwide network of business relationships.

"Alice in Wonderland on steroids! I wish Roy Williams had been my very first college professor. If he had been, everything I learned after that would have made a lot more sense and been a lot more useful... Astounding stuff."
—Dr. Larry McCleary,
Neurologist and Theoretical Physicist

"...Valuable, helpful, insightful, and thought provoking. We're recommending it to everyone we see."
—Jan Nations and Sterling Tarrant
senior managers, Focus on the Family

"Be prepared to take a wild, three-ring-circus journey into the creative recesses of the brain...[that] will change your approach to managing and marketing your business forever. For anyone who must think critically or write creatively on the job, the Wizard Academy is a must."

—Dr. Kevin Ryan
Pres., The Executive Writer

"Even with all I knew, I was not fully prepared for the experience I had at the Academy... Who else but a wizard can make sense of so many divergent ideas? I highly recommend it."

—Mark Huffman,
Advertising Production Manager, Procter & Gamble

"A life-altering 72 hours."

—Jim Rubart

To learn more about Wizard Academy, visit www.WizardAcademy.com or call the academy at (800) 425-4769